UNDERSTANDING
LOGIC
FROM BOOLEAN TO BINOMIAL

Discovering a Smarter,
More Natural Way to Think,
Compute, and Create

Kannappan Chettiar

Understanding Logic from Boolean to Binomial
© 2025 Kannappan Chettiar
All rights reserved.

This book contains original ideas, frameworks, and content developed by the author, including but not limited to:

Relational Binomial Computing System, Cognitive Numbers Theory, XY Logic, Node Fusion Technology and the Switching Battery® systems.

These are protected under copyright law and/or patents and other original intellectual property in respective jurisdictions.

This work may include content formatted or structured with the assistance of AI tools under the author's direction. All creative and legal authorship is held by the human originator, Kannappan Chettiar.

For licensing, educational use, or commercial inquiries:
kc@switchingbattery.com
www.kannappanchettiar.com

ISBN: 978-1-7378384-4-9 (Paperback)
First Edition April 2025
Printed in India

Understanding Logic

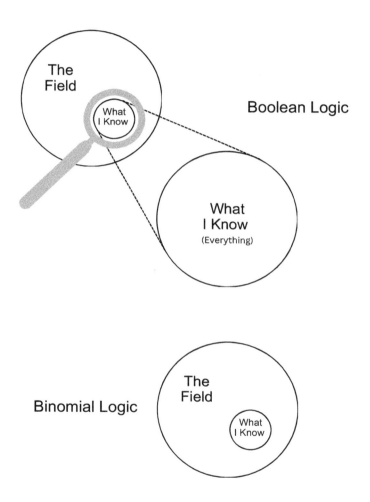

The Field

What I Know

Boolean Logic

What I Know
(Everything)

Binomial Logic

The Field

What I Know

When we stop defending what we know,
the field begins to speak.

"We did not lose truth to lies—we lost it to simplification."

To my four shining stars, Sheena, Reena, Krshant, and Veshant, whose love, laughter, and curiosity inspire me every day.

*"Boolean logic defines limits.
Binomial logic explores
possibilities."*

Contents

*"Boolean logic seeks answers.
Binomial logic seeks
understanding."*

Preface

The Sword of Solomon

There once was a king,
not remembered for power,
but for a silence that listened
deeper than law.

Two mothers came with one child—
one truth,
one lie—
and no rule could see between them.

So the king,
in calm command,
called for a sword.
"Divide the child," he said.

But this was not justice by blade—
it was wisdom in motion.
He knew the truth would speak,
not through his voice,
but through the heart that broke
to save,
not win.

And so the real mother was revealed.
Not by proof.
Not by logic.
But by relationship.

Solomon was not the judge.
He was the servant of justice.
He trusted the system to reveal
what no rigid law could hold.

So here we are,
in a digital world
built on 0 and 1,
truth or falsehood,
yes or no.
Boolean logic.

It built our machines,
our systems,
our calculations—
but not our understanding.

It cuts clean.
But sometimes,
what we need
is not a sword,
but a flow.

This book is about a new logic—
Binomial Logic,
where numbers are not endpoints,
but states in motion:

X, the known.
Y, the becoming.
Z, the field in between.

Inspired by nature,
built through the invention of the Switching Battery,
this logic listens, learns, and flows—
like rivers,
like thought,
like justice.

It is not artificial.
It is alive.

To the engineer,
the scientist,
the capitalist,
the seeker—
this is your call:

Move beyond decisions.
Enter transitions.
Let your logic breathe.
Let your intelligence flow.

Like Solomon,
may you listen deeply—
and let truth
reveal itself.

Welcome to Quantum Intelligence in a Binary World.

*"Boolean logic seeks certainty.
Binomial logic embraces
ambiguity."*

ONE

Beyond the Binary Cage

For decades, we've accepted 0 and 1 as the bedrock of digital technology. From microchips to massive data centres, we've built an empire of computation on the promise that everything can be neatly split: true or false, on or off, yes or no. This binary cage has powered revolutions in electronics, programming, and mathematics but it also hides a critical flaw.

A world of infinite nuance has been flattened into stark dichotomies. Our AI systems miss subtle context, our machines discard "unknown" inputs, and our data pipelines treat every borderline reading as a forced yes/no. As problems grow more complex—from real-time robotics to quantum-scale physics the limitations of strict 0/1 logic become more evident.

Binomial logic is a response to that reality. It proposes a new path, one that doesn't shun Boolean but expands upon it—integrating flow, context, and transformation into the very core of computation. In this chapter, we see how we got trapped in the binary cage, why it once seemed so perfect, and why the future demands a more relational approach.

1. The Binary Mindset

In a purely Boolean world, a statement is either true or false. We relish this certainty plug in the conditions, flip the gate, get an answer. This directness fueled the digital revolution, enabling:

- Speed: Logic gates run at blistering rates, toggling states in nanoseconds.
- Simplicity: On/off is easy to conceptualize and implement in hardware.
- Scalability: As we shrink transistors, we can cram more binary switches into a chip, doubling power at pace (Moore's Law).

We soared on the wings of 1s and 0s, but soared straight into problems unimagined by Boole or Shannon. The instant we ask a yes/no system to interpret fuzzy data like partial truths, probabilities, or continuous signals—binary starts to break down or requires massive kludges (like layered neural networks that approximate fluid states with countless on/off thresholds).

2. Hidden Costs of a Black-and-White World

- **Loss of Nuance**

  A reading of 49.999 might be forced to 0; 50.000 might be forced to 1—yet they're nearly identical. That single micro-difference can lead to large-scale error cascades when repeated billions of times.

- **Rigid Thresholds**

  We love thresholds in Boolean logic. Cross the line, and the system flips. But real-world signals rarely cleanly cross lines. They drift, fluctuate, or momentarily spike, leading to staccato on/off toggles that cause abrupt decisions—sometimes harmful or wasteful.

- **Data Overload**

  To mask the nuance we throw away, modern AI hoards oceans of data, hoping that raw quantity can brute-force these subtleties. This arms race in data and compute power is unsustainable—and arguably a sign that the underlying logic is insufficient.

3. The Case for Flow

In nature, transitions are rarely abrupt. A seed doesn't snap into a tree overnight; it grows. A conversation doesn't leap from greeting to deep trust in a single moment; it develops. Our binary gating fails to capture that flow between states.

Binomial logic is a step toward bridging that gap. It keeps the digital precision we value but acknowledges that input and output pass through a relational medium—Z. And that medium is not a nuisance or overhead; it's the essential place where partial truths, evolving data, and dynamic contexts converge.

4. Preview: The XYZ Triad

We can't simply declare "Stop using 0 and 1." Instead, we introduce a triad:

- X: The input not necessarily pinned as 0 or 1, but an evolving or partial state.
- Y: The output or goal, not locked to a final yes/no, but open to iterative refinement.
- Z: The crucial missing piece in Boolean logic the medium of transformation that accounts for context, flow, and real-time change.

By letting X flow to Y through Z, we stop discarding half the data or ignoring "maybe." This shift from collapse to continuum underlies the rest of the book.

5. Early Glimpses of a Better Way

Various fields have already hinted at stepping beyond binary:
- Fuzzy Logic tried to add degrees of truth.

3

- Neural Networks approximate continuous decision boundaries.
- Bayesian Methods incorporate probabilities and partial evidence.

But these are patches on top of a fundamentally binary substrate. Binomial logic aims to be more native, building from the ground up a logic that thrives on partial data and dynamic states yet still remains compatible with Boolean for simpler tasks.

6. Where We're Headed

In the coming chapters, we'll uncover how binomial logic weaves the best of Boolean's crispness with nature's fluid adaptability:

- Chapter 2 explores the historical triumph and cracks of Boolean, showing how it ascended and why it's straining under new demands.
- Chapter 3 details the core of binomial logic: how we keep synergy between knowns and unknowns, bridging them via a relational matrix.
- We'll see how Z (the so-called "missing link") reintroduces the medium that Shannon's theory insisted upon, but Boolean logic neglected.

By the end, you'll understand how Binomial logic can evolve digital systems to handle real-world complexity without drowning in brute force. Instead of fighting the unstoppable tide of partial truths, we'll flow with it—constructing computing frameworks that glean deeper intelligence from less data, respond more gracefully in real time, and unlock the 90% of nuance the binary world has historically cast aside.

TWO

Boolean Limitations

Long before computers, smartphones, or the internet, George Boole gave us a logic system that would underlie it all. In 1847, his algebra of true (1) and false (0) mapped reasoning to binary expressions. This was a game-changer for the industrial era, enabling clear, deterministic decisions in everything from electrical circuits to mathematical proofs. Over time, Boolean logic became so central that it defined how we built machines, structured code, and conceived of "logic" itself.

But the very success of Boolean logic has overshadowed its shortfalls. A system born in the 19th century is now stressed by the complexities of our 21st-century world: fluid data, uncertain conditions, and unbounded information. The cracks in the binary framework can no longer be ignored.

1. A Century of Binary Dominance

Before George Boole, logic was largely philosophical. Boole's insight that logical propositions could be written as algebraic expressions unified logic with mathematics. When Claude Shannon later showed how Boolean algebra could map perfectly onto switches and relays, the digital era began.

- Simplicity – A state can be 0 (off) or 1 (on). This reduction seemed elegant and powerful, letting us cascade decisions through gates and circuits with astonishing speed.

5

- Determinism – Boolean logic thrives on crisp boundaries. Is the voltage above a threshold? Then it's a 1. Below it? Then it's a 0.

- Scalability – Linking countless binary gates together gave birth to modern microprocessors, memory chips, and eventually the integrated systems we use every day.

This binary bedrock served well for decades, as tasks were smaller and data was simpler. But as we ventured into AI, machine learning, real-time robotics, and dynamic global networks, the rigid lines of Boolean logic began showing their cracks.

2. The Cracks Appear

As soon as conditions grow uncertain or data becomes vast and messy, Boolean logic falters. Why?

- **Rigid Boundaries**
  Boolean logic demands an immediate classification: 0 or 1, true or false. Yet many real-world scenarios exist in partial or gradient states. A sensor reading of 49.999 might be forced to "false" and 50.000 to "true," ignoring subtle difference.

- **Type I and II Errors**
  Binary thinking leads to false positives (Type I) and false negatives (Type II). In medicine, this could misdiagnose a healthy patient or overlook a serious illness. In AI, it causes constant misclassification, corrected only by brute-force data. In the legal system, the consequences are just as stark: poor individuals are often punished for minor offences, while wealthy offenders escape accountability for major crimes. Justice becomes a binary filter—guilty or not—ignoring context and inequality.

- **Discarded Nuances**
  If you only store "winning" or "losing" states, you lose everything in-between. Data that doesn't fit a rigid on/off threshold is labeled an outlier—or tossed altogether. Over time, this robs the system of
. meaningful context.

3. 0 Is Not Nothing

Boolean logic treats 0 as the negation of 1—a vacuum state, a blank. But in real systems, 0 can be a placeholder, a waiting state, or a partial capacity. It can mean "not yet," or "off until something triggers." In other words, 0 can hold potential.

When 0 is used strictly to say "false," we ignore all those possible states of "not currently active but might be relevant." Imagine a farmland left fallow—it's not "wasted," it's resting, accumulating potential nutrients for the next crop. This nuance is lost in a strict 0/1 duality.

4. The Absence of a Medium

Shannon's Information Theory emphasized that meaning emerges via a channel connecting sender and receiver. Boolean logic, though, only cares about the start (input) and end (output), ignoring the channel altogether. The logic gate is seen as an instantaneous black box.

In practice, many complexities arise inside that channel:

- Signal interference in electronics
- Context in human communication
- Evolution in AI models across time

By refusing to acknowledge the medium, Boolean logic skates over how inputs actually become outputs. It can't gracefully handle partial transformations, feedback loops, or real-time adaptation.

5. Incompatibility with Complexity

Whether it's global supply chains, autonomous vehicles, social networks, or genomic data, the challenges of the modern world involve enormous uncertainty and flux. Boolean logic's yes/no structure crumbles under these conditions:

- Binary Collapse: Forcing uncertain data into crisp categories spawns an explosion of errors and corner cases.

- Brute Force Fixes: AI tries to patch the problem by throwing more data and compute at it, but that's like building bigger dams instead of letting water find a natural route.

Nature, by contrast, is far more fluid. Systems adapt in real time, maintain partial states, and continuously reconcile new information.

6. A Bridge to Binomial

Boolean logic isn't "wrong"; it's just too narrow for a dynamic world. Its strength—binary determinism—becomes a weakness when we need to handle partial truths or evolving states.

Binomial logic offers that broader lens. By introducing a third dimension—the medium (Z)—it addresses what Boolean logic leaves out: context, flow, and real-time adaptation. Boolean logic remains in the picture—just as a simpler subset for cases where black-and-white toggles suffice.

7. The Time for Evolution

We once needed a simple logic system to make primitive computing feasible; Boolean logic fit that role perfectly. But times have changed. Data is bigger, environments are more volatile, and decisions are more

8

complex. Holding tight to purely binary frameworks is like clinging to a telegraph in an age of quantum networks.

Binomial logic isn't here to tear down Boolean logic but to evolve it nudging us from a world of forced outcomes toward a reality of fluid transformation.

In Chapter 3, we'll dive deeper into how binomial logic actually works, showing that it's more than an abstract philosophy; it's a blueprint for the next leap in real-time, relational computing.

"Truth is not what stands still—it is what flows into place when everything else moves aside."

THREE

Understanding Binomial Logic

When everything in computing is constrained by 0s and 1s, how can we deal with all the shades of reality? Binomial Logic proposes a radical, yet surprisingly natural, solution: don't force immediate decisions— allow for transformation. In this framework, the familiar binary states (true/false, on/off) become only points on a continuum, rather than the full extent of logic itself. Instead of snapping from X to Y, binomial logic recognizes the flow in between.

1. Moving Beyond Binary Boundaries

Boolean logic says: "If it's not 0, it's 1." That's neat and simple, but real processes rarely behave so absolutely. A sensor reading isn't always "low" or "high"— it could be drifting in-between. A decision isn't always "yes" or "no" —there might be an "almost," "maybe," or "let's see how events unfold."

Binomial logic allows for:

- Uncertain inputs: Instead of discarding partial data, the system carries it forward.
- Evolving outputs: Instead of a final yes/no, the result can refine itself as new information appears.
- Dynamic transitions: Rather than an instant toggle, we track how states blend and shift over time.

2. X and Y Are Not Just 0s and 1s

In Binomial logic, we still talk about input (X) and output (Y), but we don't confine them to binary extremes:

1. X (the "known" or starting condition) may represent a continuous range—like a temperature reading, a financial metric, or an AI confidence level.
2. Y (the "result" or emergent state) might be a family of possible outcomes that converge or diverge based on context.

Instead of deciding "X means Y," Binomial logic says "X flows into Y through a medium (Z), which might be partial or fluid at any step."

3. The Logic That Reflects Life

If Boolean logic is an on/off switch, Binomial logic is more like a dimmer—or better yet, a river:

- A river's source (X) merges with channels, tributaries, and varying terrain (Z).
- Eventually it reaches a delta or ocean (Y).
- Along the way, the flow rate changes, obstacles appear or vanish, and the path evolves.

This continuous, context-driven movement is how natural systems operate. Binomial logic mathematically captures this relational flow, letting partial states remain valid "midstream" rather than forcing a binary choice at every moment.

4. Preserving Unknowns and Maybes

A hallmark of Binomial logic is its preservation of unknown, interim, or borderline states. In Boolean systems, you must label an unknown piece of data or toss it out. Binomial logic:

- Holds uncertain data in the system's medium (Z), allowing it to gradually resolve or clarify.
- Adapts as fresh input arrives, so a borderline state can become more certain or pivot to an entirely new path.
- Avoids the false positives/negatives that plague strictly binary decisions by acknowledging there's more nuance than 0 vs. 1.

In practice, this means an AI or machine-learning process can function elegantly with smaller or incomplete datasets, gleaning value from partial truths rather than ignoring them.

5. Reintegration of Relationship

Boolean logic divorces variables from each other—they're toggled independently. But binomial logic reintegrates relationships:

- No variable stands alone; X influences Y, and Y can loop back to refine X if we have feedback.
- Context is everything; a single piece of data might have distinct outcomes depending on the relational constraints, expressed through Z

Imagine diagnosing an illness: one symptom doesn't strictly say "yes or no" about a disease. It contributes to a relational logic that accounts for other symptoms, medical history, and environment. The final "diagnosis" emerges from the ongoing interplay of all these factors.

6. A Simple Example

Consider a thermostat that controls heating:

- X: The current temperature reading.
- Y: The target (or set) temperature.
- Z: The operational logic—heating/cooling output, feedback from occupant preferences, even external weather changes.

In a Boolean approach, you'd set a threshold: if X < 70°F, turn the heater fully on; if X > 70°F, switch it off. That leads to constant overshoot and undershoot, a phenomenon called "bang-bang control."

In Binomial logic, the system sees temperature as flow. If X is slightly below the target, it uses partial heating slowing or stopping as it gets closer. If new data (Z) says it's windy, the system might add a bit more heat to offset drafts. You minimize abrupt toggles, preserve energy, and maintain comfort more smoothly.

7. Building on Boolean Roots

It's important to note that Binomial logic doesn't erase Boolean logic; it expands it. Boolean logic is akin to a special case where Z is fixed to force states into absolute 0 or 1. That can still be handy for simple or purely deterministic tasks. But for a dynamic, uncertain world, we want the ability to flow rather than collapse.

8. Why This Matters Now

Data Overload, Real-Time Decisions

Increasingly, we're drowning in streams of data—IoT sensors, social signals, large-scale analytics. A binary perspective discards a lot of nuance. Binomial logic is built for real-time adaptation, letting you glean insights from partial or evolving conditions without demanding all data be perfect from the start.

Complex Environments

Robotics, autonomous vehicles, global supply chains these systems can't be pinned down by static on/off thresholds. They thrive on continuous feedback loops. Binomial logic provides a structural approach for X–Z–Y flows to continuously update.

Human-Centric Interaction

Our own thinking isn't binary. We weigh possibilities, shift opinions, and refine decisions with new info. Binomial logic resonates with that process, creating user experiences that feel more natural and less rigid.

9. A Bridge to the Next Chapters

In the upcoming chapters, we'll unpack how binomial logic applies to everything from energy grids to AI, how we mathematically represent these continuous transformations, and why ignoring the medium (Z) has stunted the evolution of computing. For now, it's enough to see that Binomial logic:

- Allows states to flow continuously, rather than snapping to extremes.
- Embraces partial truths, evolving outcomes, and dynamic relationships.
- Subsumes Boolean logic rather than discarding it, preserving backward compatibility.

Next up, Chapter 4 covers the XYZ Triad in detail, showing how X, Y, and Z transform from a neat theoretical concept into a practical blueprint for building the next generation of context-aware systems.

"The problem with binary logic is not that it lies, but that it refuses to listen to anything in between."

FOUR

XYZ Triad : Input, Output, Medium

Behind every decision, every transformation, there lies a before, an after, and a means to get from one to the other. Boolean logic typically glances at the before (input) and final result (output), ignoring how the transition happens. Binomial logic brings that middle ground to life, framing all computation in terms of X (input), Y (output), and Z (the medium or transformation factor).

This XYZ Triad underpins the entire system. It says that nothing exists in isolation: you can't fully understand an outcome without grasping the path—and you can't grasp the path without appreciating the underlying input and its context.

1. X — The Known or Observed Condition

X represents what you have as a starting point:

- A measured value (like temperature or voltage).
- A set of initial conditions (like coordinates of a robot).
- A raw piece of data (like an image or a user query).

In Boolean logic, we'd treat X as a static 0 or 1. But Binomial logic acknowledges that X can hold shades of meaning partial data, multi-dimensional vectors, or continuously updating streams.

- Potential: X is often a potential input, not a forced binary.
- Evolving: X might shift over time; what was valid a moment ago

17

can morph with new data.

- Context-bound: X may carry background context. For example, a single temperature reading can mean very different things if we're talking about a baby's fever or a solar panel's surface.

2. Y—The Result, Emergent or Defined Y symbolizes where you end up:

- An output state (like an LED brightness).
- A conclusion (like a diagnosis or classification).
- A desired goal (like a final position for a robotic arm).

In Boolean logic, Y is again forced into a binary answer. In binomial logic, Y:

- May be partially formed at any point in time, converging as new elements come to light.
- Is adapting in real-time if the system is under continuous feedback loops.
- Isn't necessarily final—once we reach Y, it can become the next X for a new transformation step, enabling chained or iterative flows.

3. Z — The Medium of Transformation

Z is the missing link in standard Boolean frameworks. It's not just a single line or gate; it's the active channel that decides how X transforms into Y. Think of Z as:

- Contextual: It includes environment, constraints, user preferences, or even partial rules gleaned from machine learning.
- Adaptive: In advanced systems, Z evolves—tracking which transformations worked best in the past and adjusting to real-time feedback.

In everyday life:

- When cooking, Z is the method (baking, steaming, frying) that turns raw ingredients (X) into a dish (Y).
- In communication, Z is the language, tone, and medium that transforms a thought (X) into someone else's understanding (Y)
- In physics, Z might be a lever, gear, or field—translating force (X) into motion or energy (Y).

4. The Power of Seeing All Three

In Boolean logic, we often leap from X to Y without acknowledging Z. This omission leads to blind spots:

- Discontinuities: We skip over partial states, forcing immediate yes/no outcomes.
- Inflexibility: We can't adapt if real-time conditions shift mid-transformation.
- Data Loss: Intermediate steps vanish, losing potential insights or learning opportunities.

By contrast, Binomial logic treats X — Z — Y as a continuous or at least multi-step pathway. This is how living systems and physical processes naturally unfold.

5. Examples of the XYZ Triad in Practice

AI-Based Recommendation

- X: A user's current preferences and history.
- Y: The recommended product, song, or news feed.
- Z: The recommendation engine's algorithm—machine learning models, popularity filters, context about time of day.
- Binomial logic lets the system adapt in real time as the user interacts, rather than forcing a single static rule.

Energy Management

- X: The electricity supply at any moment (solar, wind, stored battery).
- Y: The power delivered to various loads (homes, EV chargers, grid storage).
- Z: Real-time distribution logic, factoring in weather, demand peaks, and price signals.
- The system flows from X to Y, adjusting on the fly rather than waiting for a yes/no cutoff.

Robotic Assembly

- X: The robot's current position, sensor readings about parts.
- Y: A fully assembled product or next assembly stage.
- Z: The motion planning, torque adjustments, and sensor feedback controlling how the robot transitions states.
- Instead of snapping to discrete states, the robot can micro-adjust as new data arrives, minimizing errors.

6. From Discrete States to Flow

If we rely solely on X and Y, we inevitably see discrete states: input or output, before or after. We treat the system as a black box. Z flings open that black box, revealing a continuum of small steps, partial transformations, and feedback loops. This fosters:

1. Higher Precision: Because we track more than just start and end, we can refine pathways to reduce inefficiencies.
2. Resilience: If something changes mid-flow, we adjust in real time; we're not stuck in an all-or-nothing outcome.
3. Deeper Insight: Observing how X becomes Y often yields deeper understanding of the system—potentially leading to new optimizations or discoveries.

7. Designing with the XYZ Triad

To implement Binomial logic effectively:

- Identify X: Understand what data or condition you're starting with be it partial, uncertain, or multi-sourced.
- Articulate Y: Clarify the goal or emergent result, which might remain flexible depending on real-world constraints.
- Build Z: This is the real challenge defining how transformations happen. Will it be a static rule set? An adaptive AI model? A combination of physics-based equations and real-time feedback?

A well-structured Z can handle nuance and steer partial data gracefully toward a cohesive outcome.

8. The Power of the Triad Mindset

By explicitly naming X, Y, and Z, we shift from the barebones question "How do I get from input to output?" to a richer inquiry: "What transformations, contexts, and relationships govern the journey from X to Y?"

This triad mindset:

- Helps spot lost opportunities where partial data or dynamic contexts are tossed away by binary gating.
- Encourages continuous adaptation, rather than static function calls.
- Guides us to build systems that mirror nature, where transitions are rarely instantaneous or absolute.

With the XYZ Triad in place, we're now ready to explore how binomial logic coexists with traditional Boolean frameworks—which still rule our digital hardware. In Chapter 5, we'll see how compatibility with Boolean is not only possible but a strategic advantage for bridging old systems and new paradigms.

"Truth does not live in zero or one, but in the relationship that exists between them."

FIVE

Compatibility with Boolean Logic

When a new system emerges— especially one as sweeping as Binomial Logic—the first question is whether it discards the old. In this case, the "old" is Boolean logic, the foundation of digital circuits and binary computation.The good news is that Binomial logic doesn't throw Boolean out the window. Instead, it enfolds it, treating Boolean as a useful subset or special case within a broader, more flexible structure.

1. Boolean Logic as a Subset

In Binomial Logic, X flows to Y through Z. But if you fix Z—a constant transformation that either fully blocks or fully allows the flow —then the system collapses back into a binary framework:

- Blocked state ($Z = 0$): No transformation happens; X remains inert or is considered "off."
- Allowed state ($Z = 1$): X freely becomes Y; effectively "on."

Hence, Boolean logic (0 or 1) is embedded within the X–Z–Y architecture. Binomial logic simply says: there are more possibilities for Z partial transitions, dynamic changes, or contextual influences than just 0 or 1. But if you so choose, you can pin Z to behave like a binary gate.

2. Backward Compatibility for Hardware

Modern computing hardware is built on transistors that represent bits

23

as high or low voltage. That isn't going away overnight. Binomial logic can integrate seamlessly by:

Implementing a Binomial Layer in Software

- You can wrap Boolean hardware instructions in a layer that simulates the flow from X to Y via a software-managed Z.
- This approach allows existing CPUs and GPUs to run "binomial logic" routines—no specialized hardware required immediately.

Hybrid Architectures

- Future chips could retain fundamental binary gates yet include additional binomial modules for contexts needing real-time adaptability or partial states.
- Over time, as binomial hardware matures, an increasing portion of the logic can be offloaded to specialized Z-handling components.

Thus, your legacy apps that rely on Boolean gates don't break, even as you harness binomial logic's expanded capabilities for next-generation tasks.

3. Boolean Operators Reimagined

All basic Boolean operations—AND, OR, NOT— can be interpreted as extreme cases of binomial transformations:

- AND: Requires both inputs to be fully "active." In binomial terms, Z enforces that both X inputs must align for the flow to continue.
- OR: Allows flow if at least one input is active. In binomial terms, Z merges flows from multiple Xs.
- NOT: Inverts or blocks the flow. In binomial terms, Z specifically flips X's state or denies it altogether.

By seeing these operators as special transformations in Z (constant gating, flipping, combining), it becomes clear that Boolean logic is effectively a limited binomial system lacking the capacity to represent partial or evolving states.

4. Practical Coexistence

We can imagine a tiered approach to system design:

Boolean Tier
- Fast, simple, static logic gates for tasks that are well-defined and unchanging— like integer arithmetic or known control signals.

Binomial Tier
- Higher-level modules that handle uncertain, adaptive, or context-rich operations—like dynamic resource allocation, AI inference, or real-time sensor fusion.

This coexistence ensures that classic deterministic tasks remain optimized by Boolean operations while the system can "elevate" into binomial mode for more complex needs. The result is a hybrid environment that's backward compatible yet forward-thinking.

5. Avoiding the Pitfalls of a Binary World

Boolean gates excel at clarity: they yield crisp answers quickly. But they often discard most of the contextual data in the process. Binomial logic says:

- "Yes, keep your crisp endpoints for certain tasks, but don't force everything into that Mold."
- "Use Z's relational intelligence for processes demanding nuance, partial states, or continuous adaptation."

This synergy helps us avoid re-building massive brute-force AI solutions that attempt to reintroduce the nuances Boolean discards. Instead, we handle nuance directly via binomial flow.

6. Easing the Transition

Adopting Binomial logic can be done incrementally:
- Step 1: Incorporate software libraries that model binomial transformations on top of existing hardware.
- Step 2: Migrate specific modules—like AI components or real-time control loops to a binomial approach, testing them in parallel with their Boolean counterparts.
- Step 3: Gradually extend binomial logic to more system layers, while maintaining fallback binary solutions where they suffice.

This approach ensures you neither sacrifice performance in tasks that remain well-served by Boolean gates nor miss out on the adaptability Binomial logic promises in broader contexts.

7. The Best of Both Worlds

Ultimately, Binomial logic does not seek to overthrow Boolean logic but to encompass it. Boolean logic remains unparalleled in deterministic, all-or-nothing scenarios. When the question is truly "Is the voltage above or below this threshold?" or "Is the file found or not?"— binary is ideal.

But when tackling real-world complexity—from partial truths in AI to dynamic transformations in physics—Binomial logic shows its true power. By acknowledging that 0 and 1 are just points on a continuum, we gain an architecture where Boolean logic isn't lost but becomes an elegant subset of a grander, more organic paradigm.

SIX

Mathematics of Relationship

We typically think of mathematics as a series of fixed functions $y = f(x)$. A certain input x always yields the same output y under that function. This approach has propelled us through centuries of engineering and science. Yet, real-world systems often refuse to stay pinned to a single, unchanging relationship.

Wind patterns shift. Markets fluctuate. Biological organisms grow and adapt. Boolean logic, being an extension of these static functions, crumbles under such dynamism. Binomial logic—specifically the $X - Z - Y$ framework offers a far more fluid alternative, treating relationships not as rigid lines but as ever-evolving flows of transformation.

1. The Shortcomings of Fixed Functions

Classical mathematics tells us that to find , we apply a rule f to x. But in reality:

Multiple Unknowns
- A single x might not be enough to define $f(x)$ because the path from x to y depends on many extra conditions time, temperature, user intent, etc.

Changing Functions
- What if f shifts based on context or feedback? Then the outcome no longer follows the same rule under new conditions, but classical

mathematics struggles to handle this without constant redefinition.

Exclusion of the Unknown
- Boolean logic inherits this rigidity. If an outcome isn't perfectly y or $-y$ it's seen as an error or anomaly. Large amounts of potential nuance get discarded as out-of-bounds.

In all these cases, a static function can't adapt gracefully to partial or evolving data.

2. Introducing "Z" as a Transformation Matrix

Binomial logic replaces the single function with a dynamic relationship factor Z:

$$Y = Z\,(X)$$

However, unlike a classical function, Z itself:
- Learns from past transformations,
- Modulates based on real-time context, and
- Retains partial states for future updates.

In effect, Z is a matrix of relationships not merely a single equation but a flexible, evolving set of rules. This structure allows X to become Y in ways that adapt with every iteration.

3. Flow vs. Formula

Flow-based thinking means:
1. X is not a static input but a continuous variable—often incomplete or ambiguous.
2. Z is not an unchanging function but a dynamic channel—with memory, feedback, and adaptation.
3. Y emerges not from a single pass through a fixed formula but from a cumulative, evolving process.

Consider a river's path:

- The river source (X) flows through a landscape (Z), shaping and reshaping the water's route.
- The delta (Y) is the emergent outcome, but it changes if the landscape (Z) shifts or the water's flow (X) intensifies or diminishes.

We don't just plug numbers into an equation once. We observe a continuous feedback loop the essence of binomial relationships.

4. Mathematical Tools for Binomial Logic

While the concept is broader than mere equations, we can still harness known mathematical fields:

Bayesian Inference

- Think of Z as updating its probabilities with each new observation.
- Instead of a fixed $P\ (Y\ |\ X)$ the system refines a relational distribution each time we see new data.

Eigenvector & Matrix Analysis

- In multi-dimensional spaces, transformations can be seen as matrices that rotate, scale, or distort vectors (X).
- The matrix (Z) can update in real time shifting which eigenvectors dominate, effectively changing how X maps onto Y.

Differential Equations

We can model Binomial logic as a set of coupled dynamics:

$$\frac{dX}{dt} = F(X, Z), \quad \frac{dY}{dt} = G(Y, Z), \quad \frac{dZ}{dt} = H(X, Y)$$

- Here, feedback ensures no single variable remains static. Each evolves with the others in a mutual flow.

These mathematical tools show we're not discarding formal rigor we're extending it to handle the relational and adaptive nature of real-world systems.

Preserving Intermediate States

A hallmark of Binomial logic is that we don't discard partial or evolving information. In typical binary math:
- You measure a value,
- You categorize it (above threshold = 1, below threshold = 0),
- Everything else is tossed out.

In binomial approaches, intermediate data can remain active in Z's matrix, shaping future transformations. This yields:
- Less data loss (we don't flatten nuance into yes/no),
- Fewer abrupt transitions (we adjust flows continuously), and
- Greater resilience (if new data arrives, we can pivot without re-initializing the entire system).

6. Path of Least Resistance in Equations

As we'll explore more in Chapter 8 (Path of Least Resistance Decisioning), binomial logic leverages natural flows rather than forcing binary leaps. Mathematically, this can resemble gradient descent or other optimization methods that continuously move the system to a lower-energy, lower-resistance state:

1. Compute local gradients or friction points,
2. Adjust Z to reduce that friction,
3. Recalculate in real time as X, Y, and Z remain in flux.

In practice, this approach can lead to less computational overhead than methods that rely on abrupt toggles or exhaustive searches.

7. A New Paradigm for Complex Problems

From climate modelling to genetic algorithms, from financial predictions to neural networks, a binomial approach shifts us from predefining a single function to guiding a dynamic flow. By mathematically formalizing how transformations adapt over time, we gain:

- Scalability: The system handles more variables without exploding in combinatorial complexity.
- Real-time adaptability: We don't need to keep rewriting the function; we let Z evolve with new information.

Context preservation: We hold partial states in memory, preventing the binary data "collapse" typical of older systems.

8. Toward a Unified Relational Mathematics

Ultimately, the X–Z–Y perspective hints at a unified relational math, where no element stands alone. Inputs are never just raw data—they're contextual. Outputs aren't final they're emergent. And the medium is not noise—it's the living channel that sculpts outcomes.

This is a profound shift from the classical $f(x) = y$ mindset. It's flow-based rather than formula-bound, acknowledging that every piece of data, every partial truth, and every moment of feedback matter in the evolution of a system.

Next, in Chapter 7, we'll dive deeper into Z the "forgotten medium." We'll reveal how ignoring Z has led to blind spots in Boolean logic and how reclaiming it reshapes everything from data communication to everyday decision-making.

"Truth in nature is not a declaration
—it is a discovery through
resonance."

SEVEN

Z : The Forgotten Medium

Boolean logic has fixated on input (0/1) and output (true/false) for centuries, yet it has largely ignored the question of how one becomes the other. This missing piece—the channel, context, or transformation—is the essence of Z. Binomial logic acknowledges that no transformation happens in a vacuum; there is always a medium, a relationship, a process bridging X and Y.

In everyday life, it's obvious: to get from "raw ingredients" to a "meal," you need cooking. To get from "question" to "answer," you need thinking. But Boolean logic jumps straight to yes/no, discarding the real work of transformation. Z is where that work happens.

1. Why Have We Ignored Z?

Early Simplicity
Early digital logic was about switches—electric signals toggling between off and on. This served basic computation well, so the medium of transformation was never explicitly modeled.

Overconfidence in Binary
The success of early computing reinforced the idea that "everything is either 0 or 1," dismissing the messy in-between as noise or error.

Practical Blind Spots
When you only measure inputs and outputs, you can create functional circuits, but you lose the ability to adapt to changing contexts or partial

information. This oversight once went unnoticed when computation was simpler—now it's a glaring problem in today's complex, real-time world.

2. Z as the Channel of Meaning

Claude Shannon's Information Theory showed us that information only gains meaning when transmitted and interpreted in a channel—complete with noise, distortion, and context. Binomial logic elevates that principle: Z isn't merely a channel; it's an active, adaptive medium.

Contextual

- Z shapes how X becomes Y. If Z changes, Y shifts—even if X stays the same.
- Example: In a lever (Z), the same force (X) can lift different weights (Y) depending on the fulcrum's position.

Adaptive

- In advanced Binomial logic systems, Z evolves with feedback, storing the history of transformations to refine future outcomes.
- Example: In AI, Z might be an evolving matrix that adjusts weights based on partial truths and real-world feedback, not just binary labels.

Continuous

- Rather than a static pipeline, Z is constantly in motion, factoring in new variables, changes in the environment, or learning updates.

3. Unpacking Real-World Examples

Wireless Communication

- X: The transmitted signal.
- Y: The received signal (what's actually heard).
- Z: The air (medium), complete with interference, frequency shifts, and signal distortions.

Boolean logic can't represent the distortions or partial packets that occur in flight—it only sees "packet received or not." Binomial logic can model how signals degrade or adapt mid-transmission, letting us continuously refine how X evolves en route to Y.

Fiber Optic Transmission

- X: Light pulses.
- Y: Data read by the receiver.
- Z: The fiber's physical properties, including refraction, dispersion, or even heating effects.

Instead of ignoring these "noise factors," a binomial approach integrates them into Z, allowing real-time compensation for variations in the fiber or temperature.

Decision-Making in Teams

- X: The proposal or idea.
- Y: The final collective decision.
- Z: The conversation, negotiation, and interpersonal dynamics.

Human decisions are rarely black-and-white. When a group is forced into a yes/no vote prematurely, nuance is lost. A binomial system would let proposals "flow" through the relational matrix capturing partial agreements, objections, and creative blends to produce a more evolved outcome.

4. Z as the Engine of Relational Intelligence

Traditional logic pictures X — Y as a direct mapping. Binomial logic posits that intelligence itself resides in Z—the capacity to interpret X in the context of a million subtleties:

Memory and Feedback

- Z can hold traces of past transformations. If a certain route succeeded before under similar conditions, Z reuses or refines that route.
- This is how the system learns from history, akin to how living organisms recall what worked before.

Multi-Layered

- Z isn't a single channel; it can be a matrix of partial channels. Each might handle a different factor (time, environment, complexity, preference), and they all interplay to shape the final outcome.

Fluid Decision Boundaries

- The boundaries of X and Y are not rigid walls. As Z shifts, X can morph into intermediate states before reaching Y. A single input might branch into multiple parallel transformations, with Z evaluating which path yields the best flow.

5. Recovering the Lost 90%

A striking insight from earlier chapters: Boolean logic recognizes only a sliver of reality—maybe 10% of what's truly "out there." By ignoring mediums and partial states, it discards a wealth of potential insights.

Z recovers that missing 90%. It ensures:

- Type I/II errors are not framed as "incorrect results" but seen as a function of incomplete transformations.
- Unknown or in-between states become integral parts of the process, fueling deeper adaptation.

6. Designing with Z in Mind

In building binomial systems:

Identify the Real-World Medium

- Is it physical (like air), conceptual (like a negotiation), or computational (like a dynamic matrix)?
- Model it explicitly as Z, not as a side factor.

Define Transformation Rules

- How does your system adapt when Z changes? Are you using Bayesian inference, reinforcement learning, or a custom algorithm?

Allow for Partial and Continuous Input

- Don't force X to be either 0 or 1 at any step—recognize the continuity that might exist.

Track Feedback

- Z should have a memory or pattern-recognition element so it can refine transformations based on outcomes.

7. The Key to True Adaptability

By restoring Z to logic, we:

- Gain real-time adaptability that isn't possible under strict binaries.

- Simplify complex models by letting partial states flow, reducing the data overhead that purely binary systems demand.

- Better mirror natural processes, which rarely snap from one extreme to the other, but flex and bend based on conditions.

Ultimately, Z is the forgotten medium that breathes life into logic— shifting our perspective from static inputs and outputs to dynamic, living transformations.

In Chapter 8, we see how this perspective fuels Path of Least Resistance Decisioning (PLRD), letting systems naturally find their most stable, frictionless route.

EIGHT

Path of Least Resistance Decisioning (PLRD)

One of the most powerful insights of Binomial Logic is that intelligence naturally seeks the path of least resistance. In physics, water flows downhill; electricity follows the easiest path in a circuit. In human decision-making, we often choose routes that minimize conflict or complexity. Noticeably, within Boolean constraints, we seldom capture this principle elegantly. We force decisions into discrete "winning" paths, ignoring how nature itself finds balance through gradual flow rather than sharp toggles.

PLRD—Path of Least Resistance Decisioning—bridges this gap by letting a relational logic system identify the most stable, low-friction route from input (X) to output (Y) within a given context (Z). Rather than a single, rigid answer, the system evolves toward the decision that naturally integrates all influences with minimal strain.

1. From Forced Outcomes to Natural Flows

Boolean logic approaches decisions like flipping a switch: it sets a threshold, checks if conditions exceed or fall below it, and jumps to a yes/no resolution. By contrast, PLRD says:

- Multiple pathways might exist between X and Y.
- Each path has a certain "resistance"—a measure of complexity, energy cost, conflict, or friction.

39

- The system scans these pathways continuously, steering itself toward the least resistant route.

2. How PLRD Emerges from Binomial Logic

Recall the X–Z–Y triad:

- X: Initial state or input condition.
- Z: The dynamic transformation medium, storing relational data, constraints, and real-time feedback.
- Y: The emergent outcome, shaped by how X "flows" through Z.

In a PLRD context, Z tracks not just a single transformation rule but multiple potential routes, each with its own cost or friction level. At any moment, the route with the lowest friction is favored.

Learning Through Iteration

- As the system tries different routes, it remembers which were smoother or more successful in the past.
- This memory—like a dynamic map—helps Z steer future decisions.

Continuous Recalibration

- If conditions change mid-flow, Z updates the cost of each route, allowing the outcome (Y) to shift paths in real time without discarding previous progress.

3. Measuring "Resistance"

Resistance in PLRD can manifest differently across domains:
- Energy: In physical systems, it could mean literal electrical or mechanical resistance.

- Conflict: In social or organizational decisions, it could mean the degree of disagreement or pushback among stakeholders.
- Computational: In AI or data processing, it might refer to the computational overhead or error rate associated with a particular pathway.
- Risk: In finance, it could be volatility or uncertainty.

Each type of resistance is a facet of cost, and binomial logic transforms that cost into a relational variable that shapes the flow from X to Y.

4. PLRD in Action

Autonomous Driving

- X: The car's current position, speed, sensor readings.
- Y: The target destination or immediate goal (like the next turn).
- Z: The real-time road and traffic matrix, including other vehicles, pedestrians, signals, and weather.

The PLRD approach helps the car find a route with minimal braking, minimal lane changes, and maximum safety—constantly adjusting. Instead of flipping between "go" or "stop," the car's logic flows through small, continuous course corrections.

Resource Allocation in Data Centers

- X: A set of computing tasks or processes.
- Y: The final goal: tasks completed with high efficiency.
- Z: The available servers, network bandwidth, power constraints.

A PLRD-based system identifies how to route tasks with minimal latency and energy usage. If server load spikes, the system diverts tasks to underused servers—flowing away from high-resistance paths.

Organizational Decision-Making

- X: A set of proposed strategies or changes in a company.
- Y: Implementation with employee buy-in and minimal turmoil.
- Z: The relational medium of staff opinions, budget constraints, and timelines.

Instead of imposing top-down mandates, PLRD-based logic might guide leadership to choose incremental steps that naturally gain support —adapting when resistance surfaces in certain departments.

5. Benefits of PLRD

- Efficiency: By automatically finding low-friction routes, the system saves energy, time, and resources.
- Robustness: If one path becomes blocked or costly, the system smoothly pivots to another path with minimal disruption.
- Adaptability: PLRD doesn't rely on a single "best path." It entertains multiple possibilities, letting them compete natural

In essence, PLRD transforms what is often a forced yes/no decision into a fluid optimization guided by the interplay of constraints and opportunities.

6. The Philosophical Angle: Harmony Over Force

At a deeper level, PLRD resonates with a universal principle: life seeks balance. Rivers meander around obstructions, organisms adapt to their habitats, and societies negotiate compromises. Boolean logic is about imposing a final state, but Binomial logic—and particularly PLRD—reflects the inherent intelligence of nature's flows.

By embracing PLRD:
- We honor the complexity of our systems, rather than denying it.

- We honor the complexity of our systems, rather than denying it.
- We reduce friction that arises when real-world variables are forced into abrupt toggles.
- We cultivate resilience, able to handle unpredictable shifts in conditions.

7. From Theory to Practice

Implementing PLRD in a binomial system involves:

1. Defining Resistance Metrics: Identify what constitutes "resistance" or "cost" in your domain—energy usage, social conflict, time delay, etc.
2. Equipping Z: Store these metrics and update them in real time. This might require machine learning or heuristic feedback loops that assess each micro-decision
3. Continuous Flow: Allow partial or transitional states, so the system can pivot gracefully without rewriting all logic.

As computing infrastructure becomes more distributed and data flows intensify, PLRD can serve as a cornerstone of next-generation adaptive design.

Chapter 9 will delve into how Binomial logic's real-time adaptability further extends these principles—moving beyond toggles and thresholds into a genuinely living computational framework. By letting systems flow, we unlock a world of possibilities for truly intelligent decision-making.

"In Boolean logic, the unknown is rejected. In Binomial logic, it is welcomed as a doorway."

NINE

Real-Time Adaptive Systems

The pace of modern technology demands more than raw processing power—it requires agility. As data streams swell in volume and speed, static decision rules can't keep up. Boolean logic's on/off toggles shine in stable, predictable contexts, but break under rapidly shifting conditions. By contrast, Binomial logic inherently supports continuous adaptation, preserving context even as circumstances evolve. This makes it the perfect foundation for real-time adaptive systems, where every millisecond counts and every variable matters.

1. Beyond Static Programming

A typical Boolean approach to system control:

1. Monitor inputs (A, B, C).
2. Compare each to static thresholds.
3. Trigger a fixed response (e.g., turn a valve on/off).

But in real life, conditions don't stand still. Threshold-based logic can't gracefully handle partial or emerging information:

- Abrupt changes: A single input crossing a threshold may cause the system to overcorrect.
- Slow drifts: Gradual changes often go unnoticed until a threshold is crossed, causing delayed, possibly disruptive responses.
- Compounding events: Multiple small shifts might collectively signal a big problem—Boolean logic struggles to integrate them smoothly.

Binomial systems take a more nuanced path, letting X flow to Y through a dynamic Z, continuously evaluating changes in all relevant variables and adjusting accordingly.

2. The Core of Real-Time Adaptation: Z

At the heart of real-time adaptation is Z, the medium or transformation factor. Unlike a fixed function that never changes, Z:

- Learns from previous states.
- Updates as new data arrives.
- Balances competing influences to find stable transformations.

Because Z is relational, it doesn't wait for a single binary event to decide "go/no go." Instead, it calculates how each micro-shift in X should gradually modulate Y. The result is a system that feels alive— always responding, always refining.

3. Feedback Loops in Binomial Logic

Classic control theory has used feedback loops for decades, but typically in the form of "if error > X, then correct." Binomial logic enriches this by integrating partial errors, uncertainties, and context:

Continuous Error Integration

- Rather than toggling correction on or off, the system can apply partial corrections in proportion to the detected discrepancy.
- Mistakes become catalysts for micro-adjustments that preserve overall stability.

Adaptive Gains

- In a binomial system, the "gain" or influence of each feedback

channel can dynamically shift (through Z) based on relevance.
• If a certain sensor becomes less reliable, its weight in the transformation matrix (Z) naturally diminishes.

Multiple Layers of Feedback

• You're not restricted to a single feedback path. Different aspects of Z can manage different processes, all while weaving them into a coherent X — Y transformation.

4. Applications Needing Real-Time Adaptation

Manufacturing

• A smart assembly line can calibrate robotic arms on the fly. Instead of halting production when parts deviate slightly in size or shape, binomial logic acknowledges partial deviations and rebalances Y in real time.

Autonomous Vehicles

• Road conditions, pedestrian movement, traffic patterns— everything is dynamic. A binomial-driven control system monitors a flood of sensor data (X) and recalculates the vehicle's trajectory (Y) via a constantly shifting Z. No abrupt braking from a slight sign of danger—just fluid transitions.

Financial Trading

• Markets turn volatile in an instant. Rather than buy/sell toggles, a binomial model can gradually adjust positions, factoring in continuous data about volatility, momentum, and correlated assets.

Healthcare Monitoring

- A patient's vitals (X) can fluctuate second by second. Binomial logic helps interpret micro-changes in heart rate, oxygen levels, or blood chemistry, adjusting interventions (Y) in a measured flow rather than snap decisions.

5. Resilience Through Flow

By shunning binary collapses, binomial logic yields resilience. Real-time adaptive systems that rely on flow can handle anomalies better:

- Gradual Degradation: A sensor that's drifting out of calibration won't cause abrupt logic failures. Z accounts for the drift, distributing its effects across the transformation.
- Robust to Noise: If sporadic data spikes appear, they're integrated proportionally, so the system isn't jerked into an extreme response.

This resilience translates into less downtime and fewer catastrophic failures—the system gracefully adapts instead of hitting a hard limit.

6. Designing for Real-Time Flow

Implementing Binomial logic in real-time contexts involves:

- High-Frequency Sensing: The more granular the data feed, the smoother the adaptation.
- Efficient Computations: Binomial transformations must process data in microseconds for certain applications (like high-speed robotics).
- Layered Architecture: Use multiple channels in Z, each specializing in different feedback aspects (temperature, motion, user input), merging them into a single continuous flow.

7. A New Normal for Dynamic Systems

The more we rely on automated, data-driven environments, the clearer it becomes that binary toggles can't handle the swirl of variables in play. Real-time adaptive systems need the flexible spine of Binomial logic, capable of continuous learning rather than abrupt verdicts.

By placing relationships and flow at the heart of computation, we pave the way for machines, grids, vehicles, and networks that respond more like living organisms—always in motion, always adjusting, and always ready for the next shift in conditions.

"Truth doesn't live in the answer—it lives in the relationship between the known and the unknown."

TEN

Binomial Logic Applications

Binomial logic offers a more natural and adaptive alternative to rigid Boolean systems. While Boolean logic powers basic switches and computing, Binomial logic reflects how nature actually thinks—through flow, relationships, and the path of least resistance. This makes it especially useful for building systems that are more intuitive, energy-efficient, and responsive—ideal for real-world applications like IoT, energy control, and intelligent automation.

1. Energy Systems

Energy infrastructures—particularly renewables—require continuous adaptation. Solar panels, wind turbines, and battery systems must deal with fluctuating resource inputs and unpredictable loads. Boolean logic historically handled this with binary cutoffs: on/off, charge/discharge, connect/disconnect. But nature isn't binary, and inefficiencies arise when trying to force a dynamic reality into toggling states.

Dynamic Charging and Discharging

- A binomial framework can treat battery input (X) and output (Y) not just as "charging" or "discharging," but as relational flows mediated by Z (real-time environmental conditions, usage demands, battery health).
- This allows partial charging and selective load balancing without abrupt transitions or wasted energy.

Grid-Level Optimization

- With binomial logic, power grids can adapt to changing supply and demand by modulating transformations through Z, factoring in weather forecasts, shifting consumption patterns, and variable generation.
- The result: more stable grids that use the path of least resistance to route power efficiently.

Instead of waiting until a threshold is reached to flip a switch, systems built on X–Z–Y can fluidly adjust to micro changes. This fosters higher efficiency and longevity in energy storage and distribution.

2. Artificial Intelligence

Artificial Intelligence often relies on statistical brute force, building massive models that approximate "intelligence" through layered Boolean thresholds. Binomial logic offers a more nuanced path:

Context-Aware Learning

- By embedding relationships in Z, AI can preserve partial truths and integrate them into future decisions.
- Instead of discarding outlier data as errors, a Binomial AI logic system weighs them dynamically, letting its model grow organically.

Less Data, More Understanding

- Because Binomial logic systems factor in real-time transformations, they often need smaller datasets to arrive at robust conclusions.

- This shifts AI from "bigger is better" to "smarter is better," saving on computational overhead and environmental costs.

Explainability

- Relational transitions can be traced more easily than black-box neural thresholds.
- Observers can see how X became Y through Z at each adaptive step, shedding light on the AI's reasoning process.

3. Robotics

Robotic systems demand constant feedback. A robot encountering unexpected obstacles must quickly shift tactics; a Boolean approach might freeze (0) or press on (1), but that can lead to collisions or inefficiency.

Adaptive Motion Control

- X (position, sensor data) flows to Y (target position) through Z (a real-time environment matrix). The robot doesn't forcibly choose "go/no go"—it continuously modulates its movement.
- This results in smoother navigation and fewer abrupt direction changes.

Real-Time Sensing

- Binomial logic thrives where partial or uncertain sensor readings occur.
- Instead of ignoring uncertain data or flagging it as an error, the robot treats it as a variable shaping Z, integrating it until a coherent path emerges.

Whether it's a factory line robot adjusting its grip or an autonomous vehicle weaving through busy streets, the ability to flow rather than force decisions sets binomial-driven robotics apart.

4. Financial Systems

High-frequency trading algorithms and risk assessment models typically rely on binary triggers—buy or sell, risk or no risk. But markets are complex webs of shifting human sentiment, global events, and hidden correlations.

Adaptive Risk Assessment

- A binomial framework can hold partial signals (X) and multiple potential outcomes (Y) while the market context (Z) evolves.
- Instead of toggling from "safe" to "unsafe" abruptly, the system adjusts position sizes, hedges, and strategies in fluid increments.

Smarter Trading Decisions

- Instead of chasing single threshold breakouts, a Binomial logic system accounts for momentum, volatility, and correlated assets, combining them within Z.
- Sudden collapses in logic become less frequent, reducing catastrophic trades.

Dynamic Valuation and Sentiment Mapping

- Traditional models assign fixed values to assets based on static metrics. Binomial logic, however, allows valuations to evolve as context (Z) shifts—factoring in social signals, market sentiment, and macro conditions in real time.

- An asset isn't just "undervalued" or "overvalued"—it holds potential across a range, and Binomial logic systems adjust their outlook as relationships evolve. This enables more accurate, fluid pricing and smarter timing.

This flow-based approach helps financial models handle real-time unpredictability and adapt to rare black-swan events more gracefully than strict yes/no logic.

5. Healthcare and Diagnostics

- Medical diagnostics often get forced into boolean categories: "Test is positive" or "Test is negative." That can lead to false positives, false negatives, and missed nuances. Binomial logic introduces adaptive pathways:

- Symptom Overlap: A single symptom could be part of multiple conditions. Letting $X - Z - Y$ evolve over time captures the dynamic interplay rather than a once-and-done label.

- Progressive Diagnosis: As new labs or symptoms appear, Z redefines the pathway, updating the probability of different diagnoses smoothly instead of discarding prior partial truths.

6. Communication and Networking

From wireless to fiber optics, signals must travel through mediums that distort them. Boolean logic deals with distortion by adding redundancy, error checks, and corrective overhead—often leading to inefficiency in bandwidth usage.

Binomial logic can incorporate medium awareness (Z) directly into the

communication protocol:
- Dynamic noise filtering
- Real-time channel adaptation
- Less overhead for error correction

This can improve throughput and reduce latency, especially as systems scale to billions of devices in the Internet of Things (IoT).

7. The Bigger Picture

From the examples above, a pattern emerges:
- Boolean logic collapses variables to maximize certainty.
- Binomial logic embraces complexity to find the most adaptive transformations.
- Data streams multiply and systems become more entangled, the ability to harness relationships in X–Z–Y becomes a competitive advantage. New fields—quantum computing, advanced cryptography, dynamic resource allocation—could all benefit from a logic that's not pinned down by binary constraints but thrives on relational flow.

8. Toward a Binomial World

- The hallmark of relational binomial logic is that it can handle the unknown—not just as an error or anomaly, but as part of the process. This perspective drastically changes how we design everything from microchips to macroeconomic policies. Whether it's more efficient energy grids, robots that move like living organisms, or AI systems that learn contextually without infinite training sets, binomial thinking continuously redefines what's possible.

ELEVEN

Numbers, Meaning, and Truth

At a glance, numbers appear to be the most objective tools in our intellectual arsenal—hard, quantifiable facts. In practice, numbers are anything but absolute. They gain significance only through context their application, observation, or relationship to something else. A lone number "100" by itself is meaningless until we ask: "100 what?" Dollars? Cells? Decibels?

Boolean logic has little room for such nuances. It categorizes statements into "true" or "false," collapsing numbers into discrete yes/no conditions. This approach works well for closed-form problems—like checking if a circuit is on or off—but strips away the relational meaning behind those numbers in real-life decisions. It treats all values as isolated flags rather than participants in a continuum of meaning.

Cognitive Numbers Theory

Cognitive Numbers Theory reintroduces the lost dimensionality of meaning. It's built on a foundation of Binomial logic, where numbers are not isolated symbols but self-cognitive entities—able to sense their position, adapt to context, and evolve meaning through relationship. The missing link between raw numbers and intelligent behavior is Z, the medium of transformation, which allows a number to move from the Known (X) to the Unknown (Y) through flow.

This mirrors how nature itself operates.

In the natural world, everything follows the Path of Least Resistance Decisioning (PLRD). Water doesn't choose a direction through calculation; it flows intuitively, following terrain, gravity, temperature, and space—always adapting, always optimizing.

Heaviest Sinks First, Naturally

Numbers, too, behave this way in systems not governed by rigid programming. Imagine assigning weights to the numbers 1 through 9. If dropped into the ocean, the heaviest number would sink deepest even without knowing its own weight: Number 9 might settle at the bottom, 8 just above, and so on. Number 7 would rest third from the bottom—not because of human instruction, but because the environment naturally sorts it. Meaning emerges not from computation but from position within flow.

Random Number "7" Knows Relationally

Cognitive Numbers Theory, which I developed, shows that a random number like 7 "learns" its place through interaction—through repeated sampling of its relationship with others. It doesn't need to know the full system to act; it discovers its identity over time by sensing its resistance, behavior, and outcomes. This is how numbers, when placed in an intelligent field, begin to behave like living elements.

Meaning is not imposed externally but discovered internally, through resonance. The random number 7, in such a system, behaves like a river stone—not defined by its label, but by its position among others and its resistance to flow. In this view, numbers are not static constructs—they are cognitive agents in a relational, living system. They carry memory, resistance, motion, and interaction. They become meaningful only when allowed to flow.

This is also where Binomial logic—and AI designed with it—surpasses Boolean systems. Boolean logic isolates and categorizes; Binomial logic flows, compares, and integrates.

1. Numbers as Potential, Not Finalities

This shift—from fixed logic to flow-based intelligence—marks a transformation in how we understand computation, perception, and truth. Just as a leaf does not calculate its descent but responds to the wind, so too does a number guided by flow find its rightful position—not through force, but through feedback. In this model, truth is not a binary outcome but a converging process, emerging naturally, like water finding its level.

In Boolean thinking, a numeric value is essentially data to be tested against thresholds. Is it above or below 50? Is it equal to 0? This forcibly interprets numbers in a single dimension, ignoring their broader significance.

In Binomial terms, numbers live in a flow:

- X is the raw numeric input (e.g., "100").
- Z is the transformation matrix (the conditions, context, relationships).
- Y is the emergent meaning or outcome.

Thus, "100" could represent money, temperature, probability, or something else entirely—Z decides. Instead of fixating on a single truth value (0 or 1), Binomial logic allows the system to adapt its interpretation based on the relational environment.

Seen this way, intelligence isn't unique to humans. A rock or a seed adapts—not by thinking, but by sensing and responding through repeated interaction. This is cognition too, just in a quieter form.Our evolution likely followed the same path—not by sudden design, but by deepening connections. Intelligence is not a function of neurons alone, but a universal flow—where even the smallest unit finds its place by resonating with everything around it. This is known as vibrational attunement—we all have it, and we are part of the cosmic vibration.

Where Does Meaning Reside?

If numbers themselves are neutral, then meaning arises when they interact with something larger—a context, an observer, a goal.

For instance:
- "100 miles per hour" is only "fast" if you compare it to walking speed.
- "100 dollars" is significant if you're paying for groceries, but negligible for buying a house.

Boolean logic can't capture these sliding scales of meaning. It can only say "above threshold = 1" or "below threshold = 0." But binomial logic sees meaning as an ongoing negotiation between input and context. If environmental or situational factors shift, the meaning of "100" shifts accordingly—no forced collapse into a static category.

Truth As a Relational Construct

Traditionally, truth is framed as "correspondence to reality"—if the statement matches the facts, it's true; if not, it's false. But in many real scenarios, truth emerges from how we measure, interpret, and contextualize facts.

Boolean logic limits itself to only known variables, rejecting everything outside them as irrelevant, thereby rejecting even the right answers.

Example:
- A thermometer reads 37.5°C. Is this "fever"? Boolean logic sets a threshold (≥37.5 = fever, otherwise not). But 37.5°C might be normal for one person's baseline or an imprecise reading in a hot environment.
- A Binomial logic system would not collapse the reading into "healthy or unhealthy" immediately. It would integrate context— patient history, environmental temperature, measurement accuracy —and flow toward a conclusion that might revise itself if new data appears.

Hence, truth is not a single point but a relationship among observed values, mediums of interpretation, and expected norms.

Replacing All-or-Nothing "Truth" with Continuum

Boolean logic fosters the illusion that we can decisively say "True or False," "Win or Lose," "Success or Failure."

Real systems are more complex:
- Partial truths – A system can be partially correct or hold partial data.
- Evolving truths – What was accurate under one set of conditions can drift as the environment changes.
- Contextual truths – Something "true" in one domain might be "irrelevant" or "misleading" in another.

Binomial logic addresses these complexities by integrating them into the X–Z–Y flow, where the medium (Z) tracks the factors shaping each "truth state." Instead of discarding borderline or transitioning states, the system preserves them as dynamic influences.

The Clash of Data vs. Meaning

In the modern era, we're drowning in data yet starved for meaning. Boolean logic excels at processing immense volumes of data as 0/1 flags, but it can't glean the relational insights that turn raw data into knowledge. This leads to:

- Data overload – Hordes of unfiltered bits, with minimal context.
- Blind spots – Important nuances lost, overshadowed by discrete thresholds.
- Overkill solutions – Gigantic models that try to brute-force meaning out of raw data, fueling the endless "more data, more computing power" cycle.

Binomial logic, on the other hand, suggests smaller, more context-rich data sets can be more insightful if the logic architecture is designed to embrace relationships fully.

A Bridge to Human-Like Reasoning

Humans rarely treat numbers as absolute. We evaluate them in frameworks of need, emotion, experience, or cultural norms. By adopting binomial logic, computational systems can begin to mirror that flexible approach:

- Numbers become catalysts for transformations, not final verdicts.
- Meaning arises as the system repeatedly refines relationships, guided by real-time feedback.
- Truth remains agile, open to new evidence rather than forcibly closed off.

This resonates with the human capacity for interpretation, dialogue, and learning.

Rethinking "Objectivity"

We often equate numbers with objectivity, but Binomial logic reveals that objectivity is also a process—the careful accounting of context, assumptions, and transformations. A single reading or measure can be highly subjective unless we consider how and why it was obtained. By letting X flow to Y through Z, Binomial logic systems encode the conditions that produce our so-called "objective" claims, making them more transparent and less prone to hidden biases.

Toward a Deeper Understanding

In a binomial world, the nature of numbers, meaning, and truth is multifaceted. Each is shaped by relationships, mediums, and contexts that evolve over time. This is not a rejection of rigor or clarity; it's an embrace of deeper nuance. Instead of discarding complexities, we integrate them—allowing logic to reflect the living texture of reality.

We therefore gain a system that processes:

- Numbers redefined as potential (X),
- Meaning shaped by medium (Z), and
- Truth emerging as an outcome (Y)

In Chapter 12, we'll contrast the idea of collapse (a hallmark of Boolean logic) with the concept of flow (central to Binomial logic), and see how preserving transitions over final judgments can lead to richer, more adaptive systems.

"Boolean logic sees the world as switches. Binomial logic hears the world as signals."

TWELVE

Collapse vs. Flow

Boolean logic thrives on collapse. Its power (and limitation) lies in forcing a system to choose: either 0 or 1, true or false, on or off. This binary verdict can feel refreshing in its simplicity—everything is decided, no ambiguity remains. But the modern world isn't so accommodating. We operate in the gray spaces—where partial truths, emerging states, and unknown variables persist. There's often valuable information in these in-between territories, which binary collapse discards. Binomial logic offers a different path: flow over collapse, continuum over finality.

1. What Is Collapse?

In Boolean systems:

1. You gather inputs (A, B, C, etc.).
2. A set of logic gates (AND, OR, NOT) transforms these inputs.
3. A single output emerges—1 or 0, with no shades in between.

This zero-sum resolution is what we call collapse. Once the output is decided, the system discards all intermediate or conflicting information that didn't fit the final verdict. The route is linear, the result is absolute, and any context not strictly relevant to the binary decision is lost.

2. The Cost of Collapse

- Type I and Type II Errors: Because we oversimplify, we end up

65

punishing near misses or borderline cases. Ambiguities become forced outcomes, creating false positives or negatives in fields like medicine, law, or machine learning.

- Redundant Data Requirements: To compensate for lost nuance, we often over-collect data, hoping that a bigger dataset reduces errors. This leads to massive storage and processing costs, without addressing the underlying brittleness.
- Rigid, All-or-Nothing Mindset: Binary logic simplifies complex decisions into "go" or "no-go," lacking a mechanism for weighting partial truths or uncertain states. This can cause abrupt transitions or misinformed leaps in AI systems.
- In short, Boolean logic treats the unknown like an error. But in a world brimming with complexities, that's a serious handicap.

3. The Flow of Binomial Logic

Binomial logic says: Don't collapse. Instead, flow from X to Y through Z.

- X: A starting point—an input, condition, or partial truth.
- Y: A potential outcome, but not necessarily final.
- Z: A dynamic medium or transformation factor that evolves, captures context, and adapts as new information arrives.

Rather than throwing out borderline states, binomial logic integrates them, letting uncertainty circulate until a stable relational configuration emerges. Picture a river changing course slowly over time instead of instantly halting or switching tracks.

Example:
If you have a 60% confidence in some data point being valid, Boolean logic might say "Accept it (1)" or "Reject it (0)." But a Binomial logic system can hold that 60% as an active relational state—still shaping the final decision without prematurely collapsing it to yes or no.

4. Elements in Flux

In Binomial logic, we often refer to unresolved states not as errors, but as elements in flux. Because the system acknowledges that the unknown can become known, it keeps possibilities open, leading to:

- Adaptive Computation: As conditions shift, partial information can rise or fall in significance without requiring a total system reboot.
- Reduced Data Waste: There's no scramble to gather an overwhelming dataset just to buttress an all-or-nothing decision. Partial truths can be quite informative if the system is designed to flow.
- Smooth Transitions: Instead of abrupt toggles, binomial logic can ease from one state to another, much like a dimmer switch versus a standard on/off light.

5. Avoiding Dead Ends with Feedback

In a collapse-based system, a single wrong turn can derail the entire outcome. But in a flow-based system, feedback loops can gently nudge transformations toward better alignments. Even if the system veers off course, the relational medium (Z) can redirect it back on track upon receiving corrective signals.

Practical Implication: An AI robot exploring an unknown environment might not simply decide a path is "safe" or "not safe." Instead, it grades its confidence continuously, adapting as new sensor data arrives. That means fewer disastrous "wrong collapses" and more nuanced maneuvering.

6. Harnessing the Flow in Real-World Systems

Healthcare Diagnostics
Rather than labeling a patient's state as "healthy" or "diseased," a binomial system keeps symptoms, lab results, and expert opinions in flow, integrating them as they develop.

Financial Forecasting

Rather than forcing buy/sell toggles, the market data streams into a Binomial logic matrix, shifting projections dynamically and avoiding sudden collapses when conditions change.

Climate Modeling

Rather than deterministic yes/no thresholds on emissions or temperatures, binomial logic merges numerous interdependent variables in real time, producing continually refining predictions rather than locked-in ones that ignore new data.

7. The Future of Flow

Cultures, organisms, and phenomena all flourish in the space between extremes. Flow-based computing aligns with how nature itself evolves, bridging the gap between static and adaptive.

By learning to see the world as relationships in motion, we gain the resilience and intelligence we need for ever-increasing complexity. Collapse has served us well, simplifying the early days of digital electronics. But as we move into an era of real-time data floods, quantum computing horizons, and machine minds that must learn like living systems, the old toggles can't keep up. Flow-based binomial logic steps in—preserving nuance and channeling it into ever smarter, more fluid operations.

In Chapter 13, we explore patterns, shapes, and time as living examples of binomial flow—where continuous transitions redefine everything from geometry to temporal dynamics. The world may never have been binary, after all.

THIRTEEN

Patterns, Shapes, and Time

Throughout this book, we've traced how Binomial Logic redefines the fundamental building blocks of computation, shifting from static binaries to fluid relationships. But the real power of this approach is most evident when we step into the domains of patterns, shapes, and time—the very fabric of physical reality.

Boolean logic, at best, provides snapshots: 0 or 1, discrete steps, forced states. The natural world, however, is brimming with curves, cycles, rotations, and continuous evolutions whether it's the spiral of a galaxy, the waveform of a heartbeat, or the elliptical paths of planetary orbits. Binomial Logic reclaims the relational flow that underpins these shapes and sequences.

1. Patterns as Emergent Relationships

In traditional computation, pattern recognition is often an exercise in segmentation: chunking data into discrete blocks, then matching those blocks against a pre-existing library of shapes or templates. This approach works well enough for simpler problems (like recognizing typed letters), but stumbles when faced with naturally fluid or partially unknown forms—think of a swirl of leaves in the wind.

Binomial Logic, however, sees patterns as continuous transformations:
- X might be the initial form or state (like a single leaf position).
- Z is the dynamic environment (wind currents, temperature, turbulence) that modifies the leaf's path.

- Y is the emergent arrangement—no longer a fixed "final shape" but a shifting pattern revealed over time.

Because Z encapsulates context and flow, the system can detect patterns as they emerge, not just after they've locked into a final position.

2. Shapes Beyond Binary Steps

Geometric figures circles, spheres, spirals, and more are notoriously difficult to capture with purely binary logic. If you try to draw a circle using Boolean increments, you end up with pixelated approximations. The more precision you need, the more microunits you must subdivide and your data load balloons without truly capturing smooth curvature.

In Binomial Logic:
- We don't approximate a circle via stepwise increments.
- We let X flow to Y along a least-resistance path determined by Z.
- The circle becomes a relation (distance, angles, continuity) rather than a set of disjointed coordinates.

This continuous approach yields a shape that is mathematically "cleaner" and more resource-efficient to compute. Instead of storing each microscopic point on the curve, you store the relational rule—and let the system adaptively fill in the rest.

3. Time as a Transformational Dimension

Time has long been treated as a separate parameter in computations— an outside clock ticking forward in discrete increments. But in many natural and physical processes, time is an intrinsic aspect of how states evolve.

From a binomial perspective, time is deeply intertwined with Z:
- X at one moment flows to Y at the next, through the evolving constraints and opportunities of the medium (Z).
- The system can track progression without forcing external time

steps, effectively letting time emerge from the relational changes themselves.

This is akin to how relativistic physics views time: not as a universal constant but as something shaped by velocity, mass, and gravitational field (which we can treat as forms of Z). We no longer see time as a mere sequence of t=0, t=1, t=2; we see it as part of the transformational matrix that turns one state into another.

4. Path of Least Resistance Decisioning (PLRD)
Many natural shapes—like the spiral of a galaxy or the swirl of water down a drain—reflect the principle of least resistance decisioning, PLRD. They organize themselves according to energy gradients, flow constraints, and environmental forces. Boolean logic can't easily encode "least resistance" because it reduces direction and force to basic toggles.

Binomial systems elegantly encode it:
  * X might be a set of initial conditions (mass, velocity, position).
  * Z captures the forces or mediums at play—gravity, friction, density.
  * Y is where the entity ends up, with the shape of its path revealing the path of lowest energy or least resistance.

By allowing each moment to dynamically refine the relationship, you see emergent shapes (spirals, waves, fractals) naturally, rather than forcing them through discrete simulation steps.

5. Implications for Modeling and Simulation

Efficiency Gains
Instead of incrementally simulating every microstate in a fluid or a chaotic system, you let binomial logic define the transformation. This can drastically reduce computational overhead, because you store relationships—not exhaustive states.

Real-Time Adaptation

As conditions change mid-simulation, you don't have to reset or forcibly recast the entire system. Z adapts on the fly, rerouting the path from X to Y as new conditions emerge.

Natural Patterns in AI

For AI tasks like handwriting recognition, voice analysis, or dynamic gesture control, a binomial framework can treat patterns as continuum rather than discrete frames. That means less data-laden training, fewer classification errors, and more nuanced interpretation of fluid human inputs.

6. Embracing the Flow

If Boolean logic is a series of rigid snapshots, Binomial Logic is like a movie reel that never stops. Each frame merges into the next, shapes continuously morph, and time breathes through everything. We're no longer bounding patterns with artificial edges; we're witnessing how shapes, structures, and even temporal sequences emerge from dynamic relationships.

When we accept that patterns, shapes, and time are not static objects but relational constructs, we're freed from the tyranny of stepwise approximation. Instead, we dive into the flow—and from that vantage point, we can build systems that more closely mirror the living, evolving universe.

In Chapter 14, we'll shift focus to how this "relational mindset" transforms AI itself—pushing from brute-force, deterministic approaches to a new era of adaptive, context-driven, and fundamentally binomial intelligence.

FOURTEEN

Deterministic to Relational AI

Modern artificial intelligence often wears the veneer of complexity—millions of parameters, deep neural layers, and sprawling data sets. Beneath this complexity lies a familiar core: deterministic computing steps that rely on Boolean or numerical thresholds. We feed these systems massive amounts of data, tune their weights, and hope statistical generalization will yield insights akin to true intelligence.

In Boolean logic, A and B are treated as separate variables connected by rigid operands like AND, OR, and NOT—evaluated in isolation without regard for deeper meaning. In contrast, XY logic treats A and B together as a unified whole under X (the Known), and explores their transformation into Y (the Unknown) through Z, the medium of flow. Here, the relationship between X and Y is essential—unlike Boolean logic, which ignores all context outside its predefined conditions.

The Limits of Determinism in AI

1. Brittle Boundaries
Traditional machine learning processes data through fixed pipelines. Even with advanced techniques like backpropagation, each layer produces outputs that are essentially pushed into discrete yes/no gates. The moment an input strays from the training distribution, the model's predictions can go catastrophically wrong. There's no built-in mechanism for relational "give" or "adaptation" in the moment—just an approximation learned from historical data.

2. AI Arms Race

Because Boolean-based or purely numeric systems disregard the majority of contextual nuances, AI models compensate by devouring enormous data sets to spot patterns. This leads to the well-known AI arms race: bigger servers, bigger networks, bigger everything. Yet more data isn't necessarily better intelligence—it's just more fuel for a fundamentally rigid logic engine.

3. Static Decision Thresholds

In typical neural networks, decisions boil down to whether activations exceed certain thresholds. The thresholds may be learned, but they're still effectively binary triggers once set. This can't replicate the continuous flow of reasoning humans use when faced with ambiguous or evolving conditions.

Enter Relational Binomial Logic

Rather than treat intelligence as a chain of deterministic steps, Binomial logic asserts that all transformations happen in a relational medium—Z —where unknowns are not shoved into the nearest box, but used as fuel for adaptation.

- X: Input data or raw sensory information
- Y: Emergent output or decision
- Z: The adaptive transformation that modifies how X becomes Y, in real time

This X–Z–Y triad naturally accommodates continuous updates. If new data arrives mid-processing, the system can reconfigure Z, reweighing outcomes without forcibly discarding partial states. Where deterministic AI "snaps" to a final answer, relational AI flows toward it, preserving context along the way.

Context as a First-Class Citizen

Conventional deterministic AI may attempt to "learn context" by embedding a statistical representation of it in hidden layers. Relational AI, built on binomial principles, acknowledges that context is the medium—a living part of the logic. This changes the flow:

1. Interpretation – Instead of jammed thresholds, a relational model looks at how each new piece of information shifts the current transformation matrix Z.
2. Integration – Unknowns aren't placeholders for "missing data"; they become real-time factors shaping how X transitions to Y.
3. Iteration – The system remains in flux until a meaningful resolution emerges, not because it's forced to finalize, but because the relationships converge on a coherent outcome.

This stands in stark contrast to binary-based AI, which must fix its thresholds and operate in sequential, yes/no steps.

Less Data, More Wisdom

Relational Binomial Computing Systems tend to need less raw data because they rely on smarter transformations. When Z can adapt in real time and store partial relationships, you don't need to see a million nearly identical examples to "figure out" the pattern. The system self-tunes, bridging knowledge gaps on the fly.

As a result:

• Smaller training sets can yield strong performance if the transformation space (Z) is robust.
• Rare events or anomalies are integrated without requiring the model to artificially retrain on edge cases—Z reconfigures in response to the event.
• Human-like inference becomes possible, where intuition isn't about memorizing every path but about recognizing subtle relational cues.

Implications for the Future of AI

1. Adaptive Autonomy – Robots or systems that can handle unexpected changes in real environments without grinding to a halt.
2. Explainability – With a relational architecture, the path from input to output can be traced through Z's adaptive steps, making the black box more transparent.
3. Scalable Complexity – Instead of building billion-parameter models, we focus on building a sophisticated Z structure that can adapt quickly, cutting down on computational waste.

Deterministic AI views the world as static data points, forcing them into predetermined curves. In contrast, Relational AI engages with the world as a dynamic dialogue, where context is king, unknowns hold hidden value, and intelligence emerges from bridging these complexities.

By recognizing that binary 0/1 choices are just a small part of a broader relational landscape, we're moving beyond pursuing ever-larger models to cultivating more profound, nuanced logic. This fundamental shift transforms our approach from deterministic training to relational learning, redefining the very fabric of artificial intelligence.

The implications are profound: we're evolving from reliance on massive Large Language Models (LLMs) to the precision of Small Data Predictive Models (SDPM).

FIFTEEN

Relationship and Intelligence

Intelligence has often been described as the ability to acquire and apply knowledge. Yet the dominant approach in computing has been brute force—loading massive datasets, training colossal AI models, and hoping that sheer volume compensates for a fundamental gap in logical structure. As we've seen, Boolean logic forced the world into binary boxes, ignoring the relational subtleties that foster genuine understanding.

Binomial logic reopens the door to those subtleties. It suggests that intelligence is not a product of raw data alone, but of how data flows through context, how input and output relate in real time, and how unknowns are integrated instead of discarded.

Relationship as the Core of Knowledge

At its heart, knowledge is relational. A fact gains meaning only when connected to a broader framework—a place, a time, a cause, a purpose. Traditional computing tries to fix data points into 0/1 states, but that robs them of the fluid interplay that sparks insight.

1. Contextual Ties

- In a Binomial logic systems, X evolves into Y through Z—the channel that captures historical patterns, environmental feedback, even emotional or situational cues.
- This means no data stands alone; it's always interpreted through a matrix of relationships.

2. Dynamic Learning
- Boolean logic typically sees learning as recalibration, applying a new set of yes/no rules.
- Binomial logic treats learning as a continuous flow, where every transformation adjusts how X and Y relate for future scenarios.

3. Intelligence Beyond Brute Force
- Learns from less data – Because relationships capture nuance without forcing everything into discrete bins, fewer examples may be required to attain high accuracy.
- Adapts in the wild – Instead of needing a fixed training cycle, a Binomial logic system evolves as it encounters new states, refining Z in real time.
- Preserves partial truths – It doesn't discard borderline cases or unknown inputs but uses them to shape and expand its relational models.

In essence, Binomial logic doesn't just memorize answers; it discovers how transformations unfold in different contexts.

Human-Like Insight
If you asked a human to navigate an unfamiliar city, they wouldn't rely on a 0/1 map. They'd observe, compare, adjust. They'd note landmarks (X), interpret the route's conditions (Z), and aim for a destination (Y) with continuous adaptation. This is a relational process no single step is truly "right" or "wrong," but each informs the next.

Binomial logic resonates with human cognition because it:
- Recognizes gradients of truth or accuracy.
- Incorporates past outcomes into future decisions.
- Thrives on flow instead of collapse.

By formalizing that relational essence in code and circuits, we bring computing logic one step closer to organic intelligence.

The Myth of Perfect Consistency

Boolean systems promise consistency once something is declared 1, it stays 1. But real intelligence often lives in organized chaos, balancing contradictory pieces of information until clarity emerges.

- Binomial logic accommodates that dance. X might be 90% certain in a given context, or it might oscillate until Z stabilizes into a workable output.
- This is not indecision or error—it's how living organisms weigh possibilities before acting.

Paradoxically, by allowing temporary ambiguity, a binomial system reduces overall error. It ensures fewer forced collapses into an incorrect binary state.

Reintegration of the Unknown

Perhaps the greatest hallmark of intelligence is comfort with the unknown—the ability to explore, hypothesize, and refine. Boolean logic had no place for unknowns; it forced them into the nearest available box (0 or 1).

Binomial logic reserves infinite room for what isn't fully understood yet:

- Z can expand as a set of sub-transformations, each exploring a different angle.

- The system can hold multiple possible pathways simultaneously until evidence clarifies which is more likely.

- Ultimately, the unknown isn't suppressed—it's reclaimed as part of the relational fabric.

A Future of Relationship-Centric Computing

Reclaiming intelligence through relationship means building technologies that:

- Respond to real-time context rather than static rules.
- Integrate partial information instead of discarding it.

From self-healing networks that adapt to changing loads, to AI health assistants that weigh nuanced symptoms, binomial logic sets the foundation for machines that think in flow.

In the next chapter, we'll see how these principles aren't confined to IT or hardware alone. They resonate with deeper ideas about consciousness, natural law, and the fabric of reality—leading to implications that reshape how we view not just computing, but life itself.

SIXTEEN

Natural Law and Consciousness

Binary logic has served as a reliable workhorse for centuries, fueling revolutions in electronics, communication, and data processing. But the introduction of Z—the medium or transformation factor—expands our view of what computation can be. It also invites questions that reach beyond conventional engineering and into the realms of consciousness and natural law.

The Question of "Medium" in Conscious Systems

When we say X transforms into Y via a medium Z, we imply that there is a context, environment, or relational substance where this transformation unfolds. In living systems, you might call this medium mind, awareness, or consciousness—the intangible field within which perceptions become decisions, and experiences become meaning.

- In neuroscience, signals (X) become behaviors (Y) through neural networks (Z).
- In psychology, stimuli (X) become thoughts or feelings (Y) through an internal mental framework (Z).
- In spiritual traditions, intentions (X) manifest outcomes (Y) through an unseen energetic or consciousness-based medium (Z).

The concept of Z reframes these diverse explorations under a single relational principle: transformation is always contextual.

If consciousness is the ultimate medium through which data (X) becomes interpreted truth (Y), then binomial logic might be the closest computational analogy to how minds actually work: not by toggling "on/off," but by adapting, relating, and evolving.

Reintegrating Science and Philosophy

Historically, Western science separated itself from metaphysical questions, focusing on measurable phenomena. Yet quantum mechanics, complexity theory, and now Binomial logic suggest that the boundary between matter and meaning is far thinner than we once believed.

- Quantum entanglement shows that particles don't merely exist in isolation; they relate through a hidden medium.

- Complex systems demonstrate emergent behavior that can't be predicted by linear cause-and-effect.

- Relational Binomial logic posits that no input is ever alone; it transforms via a medium that might be physical, informational, energetic, or even conscious.

This doesn't mean Binomial logic proves metaphysical claims. Rather, it offers a framework for bridging the gap between hard science and philosophical inquiry by formally acknowledging a relational factor (Z) that shapes outcomes.

Natural Law Revisited

Natural law typically refers to the underlying principles governing reality—be they physical laws (gravitation, electromagnetism), biological imperatives (evolution, homeostasis), or moral and ethical constructs (justice, rights). In all these realms, we see patterns of transformation, not just binary states.

1. Physical Laws

Newton's laws, Einstein's equations, and even quantum fields can be interpreted as transformations of X into Y (mass, energy, momentum) modulated by a relational constant or matrix (Z). Binomial logic mirrors these relationships by letting Z remain dynamic—capable of shifting based on context or scale.

2. Biological Imperatives

Life thrives on feedback loops, resource flows, and adaptive strategies. Genes (X) become traits (Y) through an environmental medium (Z). Binomial logic resonates with this flow-based understanding of life, as it natively integrates feedback and transformation in its formalism.

3. Ethical and Moral Constructs

Ethical decision-making is rarely a simple "yes/no" scenario. Context, cultural norms, empathy, and outcomes all shape decisions. Binomial logic suggests that morality (Y) arises from inputs (X) through the cultural or situational medium (Z). This explains how one action can be seen as virtuous in one context and questionable in another—because Z changes the transformation.

Consciousness as the Ultimate Z?

If we speculate that consciousness could be the medium itself—an omnipresent field within which all transformations happen—then Binomial logic becomes almost a computational reflection of that universal principle.

- It does not reduce experience to 1 or 0.

- It holds space for transitions, possibilities, and unknowns.

- It treats relationship as fundamental, mirroring how conscious experience is relational: we perceive through senses and interpret through mind.

This is more than poetic musing. As we push toward AI that exhibits broader forms of intelligence, it's plausible that a binomial architecture, which honours relational states, might better simulate consciousness than purely binary or even fuzzy logic could. The more our machines operate via dynamic contexts, the more they mirror the behaviour of conscious systems, bridging that intangible gap between living awareness and mechanical computation.

Where Does This Lead Us?

1.Unified Perspectives
Binomial logic might serve as a common language for integrating scientific laws, engineering principles, and philosophical debates about the nature of reality.

2.Enhanced AI and Cognitive Models
By adopting a relational architecture, future AI might exhibit emergent features akin to self-awareness or at least deeper contextual understanding.

3.Moral and Ethical Computing
Systems that don't discard nuance can make decisions that are more equitable, flexible, and harmonious with diverse ethical frameworks.

4.Reevaluation of 'Natural' vs. 'Artificial'
The line between natural and artificial intelligence blurs when we adopt the same relational logic for building machines that living organisms evolved through countless iterations.

The Road Ahead

Just as quantum mechanics forced physicists to rethink classical assumptions, Binomial logic forces us to question the binary underpinnings of our digital age.

Consciousness, ethics, and natural law all push against the boundaries of science. By adopting a logic that values medium as much as input or output, we unlock possibilities that remain stifled in purely binary frameworks.

- Will binomial logic yield breakthroughs in theories of consciousness?

- Could it reconcile moral relativism under a dynamic but structured computational lens?

- Might it unify disciplines from physics to philosophy, all sharing a common relational language?

We don't yet know. But the potential is vast and the door is now open.

In the final Chapter 17, we'll conclude our journey by looking forward:

- How do these binomial principles reshape our collective future?

- Where does relational computing lead us and what might be the broader implications for a world ready to move beyond the binary cage?

"To discard a partial truth because it isn't whole is to walk away from a path just before it opens."

SEVENTEEN

The Future Is Binomial

Binary logic has fueled our progress for centuries, culminating in a global digital infrastructure that touches every aspect of modern life. But as we face complex challenges—climate change, quantum frontiers, real-time AI, and hyperconnected systems—we increasingly feel the friction of forcing the world into 0 or 1. The cracks are showing. The question is no longer whether Boolean logic will adapt; it's how we'll transcend its limits.

Not a Death Sentence for Binary

This isn't the end of Boolean logic—far from it. Even in a Binomial world, the binary still has a place: it can handle straightforward, deterministic tasks with unparalleled efficiency. But for tasks that demand context, fluidity, and continuous learning, the binary yes/no framework is insufficient. Binomial logic emerges as a natural evolution, not a replacement.

Think of it as upgrading from a simple two-speed bike to a multi-gear machine. We're not throwing out the old model; we're expanding it so we can tackle more diverse and treacherous terrain without wearing ourselves out in the process.

A Shift from Collapsing to Flowing

The core strength of Binomial logic is its ability to flow rather than collapse. It refuses to discard "almost," "maybe," and "still unknown." Instead, it integrates them as opportunities for adaptation.

Where Boolean logic sees an endpoint, Binomial logic sees a transformational:

- X isn't just a static 0 it's a state of potential.
- Y isn't a final 1 it's an emerging outcome.
- Z, the oft-overlooked medium, orchestrates how X becomes Y, enabling real-time shifts in meaning and structure.

This triad allows a system to learn from each transition, refining and reconfiguring its own processes as it goes. It's logic that breathes.

Universal Applicability

From the vantage point of these final pages, it's clear that Binomial logic transcends any single technology or discipline:

- Energy Systems become adaptive, with parallel and series flows coexisting for optimal efficiency.
- AI Models harness real-time relational data, drastically reducing the need for brute-force learning.
- Robotics moves from rigid pre-programmed routines to fluid, context-aware motion that's more in line with living organisms.
- Finance and Economics gain predictive resilience, factoring in volatility, feedback loops, and continuous updates without forcing discrete buy/sell triggers.
- Biology, Medicine, and Neuroscience discover a computational language that more closely mirrors the synergy of living systems.

No matter the domain, the principle is the same: harness the constant interplay between known and unknown, letting context (Z) drive the transformation from input (X) to output (Y).

Collaboration with Human Insight

Perhaps most exciting is the synergy between human cognition and binomial logic. The human mind rarely thinks in strict 0/1 terms; it continuously negotiates degrees of confidence, potential, and context. Binomial computing echoes this pattern, making technology more intuitive, less error-prone, and deeply co-creative with us. By embedding relational intelligence into our systems, we reduce the jarring dissonance between how we think versus how our machines think. This closeness means fewer illusions of "black box AI" and more coherent, transparent interactions between human insight and machine processes.

Next Steps and Open Invitation

This book has introduced the framework, mathematics, and potential applications of the Relational Binomial Computing System. But these chapters are only a starting point. The real transformation will happen as communities of researchers, engineers, entrepreneurs, artists, and thinkers take these ideas and build on them—expanding the code libraries, forging new hardware architectures, and experimenting across fields.

- How will we design truly binomial-based chips?

- Can we unify quantum entanglement (arguably another relational phenomenon) with Binomial logic?

- Will dynamic AI driven by X–Z–Y logic outcompete the largest brute-force models that rely solely on scaling up parameters?

We don't have all the answers. But that's the point: Binomial logic thrives on not knowing, on adapting, on constantly refining its own rules. It's a living logic in a living world.

A New Era in Computation

By recognizing that 0 and 1 are not endpoints but moments in a flow, we reclaim the vast middle ground where real intelligence resides. Boolean logic isn't obsolete—it's simply incomplete. In the same way that Newtonian physics gave way to relativity and quantum mechanics without losing its practical utility, Binomial logic stands ready to augment and expand what binary once started.

The future is binomial because the future is fluid, interconnected, and infinitely creative. In that future, we'll continue to code our systems—but we'll also co-evolve with them, forging decision-making processes that are as alive and adaptive as the world they inhabit.

- Binary was our spark. It led to Artificial Intelligence (AI).

- Binomial is our current. Leading to Quantum Intelligence (QI).

This is just the beginning.

Binomial Logic Is Not Truth

"Truth is not what we force into form, but what flows into place when everything else steps aside."

In this book, Binomial logic is presented as a powerful framework—but let us be clear:

- It is not the truth. It is the vessel that allows truth to emerge.

Think of truth as water. It flows, shifts, and responds to context. It resists containment, yet seeks coherence.

Now, think of Binomial logic as the riverbed—the structure or vessel that shapes how that truth moves, how it's discovered, and how it's shared.

- Boolean logic tries to dam the river: 0 or 1, true or false. It demands finality, even when the truth isn't ready.

- Binomial logic opens the terrain. It allows truth to move, to resonate, to find its level.

Binomial processes ambiguity, preserves partial truths, and lets context guide understanding.

This doesn't make Binomial logic better than truth—it simply aligns more closely with how truth behaves in the real world.

In the end, Binomial logic doesn't replace truth. It respects it.

It holds the space for it to unfold—patiently, relationally, and without force.

Binomial Logic in Action
A Companion Section of Real-World Case Studies

This section is designed as a hands-on companion to the main chapters of this book.

The Relational Binomial Computing System is a proprietary innovation, safeguarded by intellectual property laws. What you've just encountered is not a static model—but a living, adaptive framework. The following case studies reveal how it functions across diverse domains, including energy systems, AI, robotics, finance, computing, and even everyday tools. You'll meet a self-aware number and discover how platforms like Arduino can be taught to think in binomial terms—replacing rigid logic with relational intelligence.

Each case is written not only to explain, but to invite experimentation. These are not rigid templates, but playgrounds for logic in motion. Try adapting them to your context—whether you're an engineer, student, educator, or curious mind.

The goal is not complexity—it's clarity through flow.

Let the logic unfold. Let the patterns reveal themselves.

Above all, enjoy the process of thinking, building, and seeing the world a little differently.

Welcome to Binomial Logic in Action.

Let's begin.

"Truth in nature is not a declaration—it is a discovery through resonance."

Energy Systems

Overview

Modern energy systems contend with fluctuating renewable inputs sunlight and wind are inherently variable. Traditional solutions rely heavily on binary switching (on/off, charge/discharge, series/parallel) to manage this variability. While workable in small-scale setups, these binary transitions can introduce inefficiencies, abrupt load changes, and the need for extra hardware to handle balancing and safety.

Binomial logic enables smooth energy management—X (input) draws raw power, Y (output) delivers usable power, and Z (matrix) dynamically adjusts states to optimize balance, storage, and supply.

Implementation

Input (X)

- This input is the raw, potentially fluctuating DC output from solar panels, wind turbines, or other generators.
- Because conditions (sun intensity, wind speeds) change throughout the day, X is anything but a stable 0 or 1.

Transformation (Z)

- A software/hardware control layer tracks factors like battery voltage levels, real-time demand, and external conditions such as temperature or peak consumption hours.
- Z enables dynamic partial states—modules can charge, discharge, or reconfigure in parallel/series as needed.

- Adaptive switching enables smooth transitions—some modules stay in parallel for balance, while others shift to series for power, avoiding rigid charge/discharge modes.

Output (Y)
- The net result is a stable, reliable power output that aligns with both the demand side and the system's internal optimization goals.
- Y isn't simply "power delivered" or "battery charging," but a dynamic blend of multiple states that changes fluidly over time.

Results and Benefits

Energy Efficiency
By matching the partial states to real-time generation, the system harnesses more usable energy and avoids high frequency switching losses.

Less Hardware Overhead
With dynamic parallel-series coexistence, balancing hardware and complex charge controllers can be simplified or integrated into the main control logic.

Extended Battery Life
Fewer abrupt transitions reduce stress on battery cells, leading to improved longevity and less capacity fade over time.

Scalability
The same approach scales from small residential solar arrays to large commercial wind-solar hybrids, adjusting internal logics in proportion to system size.

In short, Binomial logic transforms energy management from rigid binary steps to a flow-based architecture. By adapting switching states continuously, the system optimizes power usage, reduces wear, and integrates with fluctuating renewables in a far more harmonious and efficient manner.

Artificial Intelligence

Overview

Most AI systems rely on binary or threshold-based logic under the hood: neural network activations become "on/off" at certain thresholds, classification tasks force discrete labels, and uncertain data points get pushed to one side or the other. This approach can be brittle requiring huge datasets to smooth out inevitable edge-case errors and lacking a clear strategy for handling partially known inputs.

Binomial logic reimagines AI as a flow of continuous transformations rather than a chain of discrete gates. Input data (X) might be sensor readings or user queries; the output (Y) might be a classification or recommendation. The transformation matrix (Z) tracks real-time changes and partial understanding, adapting itself with each new observation rather than demanding a final yes/no resolution.

Implementation

Input (X)

- Could be text, images, time-series sensor data, or any mix of structured/unstructured streams.
- Unlike strictly binary pipelines, X can hold partially classified items or ambiguous features without forcing an immediate final decision.

Transformation (Z)

A dynamic layer that fuses multiple learning techniques:
- Bayesian inference for probabilistic updates,

- Reinforcement signals that tweak model parameters mid-process,
- Adaptive weighting that learns to trust certain feature sets more over time.

Z allows the system to carry incomplete evidence along, refining it continuously.

Output (Y)

- Y represents the evolving prediction or action, not just a one-shot classification.
- In simpler tasks (like spam detection), the model might converge quickly to a "likely spam" outcome. For more complex data (like image scenes with partial visibility), it can keep refining the output as new frames or context appear.

Results and Benefits

Reduced Data Requirements

By leveraging partial truths and updating them in real time, the system extracts more insight from smaller datasets. It doesn't discard borderline examples as noise or train extensively to handle outliers.

Improved Explainability

Observers can look inside Z to see how each chunk of evidence shifted the final outcome, rather than scanning opaque, all-or-nothing activations.

Robust to Novelty

Data points that don't fit existing classes aren't hard failed; they flow through Z as "unknown" states until the system either learns a new category or merges them with existing patterns.

In essence, Binomial logic breathes flexibility into AI, replacing the stark edges of binary classification with context-aware transitions. Systems become both more data-efficient and more responsive, offering a path to truly adaptive intelligence instead of brute-force categorization.

Robotics

Overview

Traditional robotic control often relies on threshold-based triggers: If sensor data crosses a limit, the robot either stops or takes a predefined action. This can result in abrupt manoeuvres, clumsy obstacle avoidance, and high rates of recalibration. As environments grow more dynamic—crowded factory floors, unpredictable terrains—binary logic struggles to keep pace.

Binomial logic offers a continuous approach. Instead of flipping from "move" to "stop," the robot interprets sensor readings (X) through a relational transformation (Z) to produce adaptive motor commands (Y). By preserving partial signals and intermediate states, the system moves more fluidly and reacts gracefully to emerging conditions.

Implementation

Input (X)
- Data from LIDAR, cameras, ultrasonic sensors, or force/torque sensors on robotic arms.
- Rather than a single yes/no for obstacle presence, X can store partial confidence levels, incomplete scans, or uncertain distances.

Transformation (Z)
- A real-time control layer that merges sensor feedback with learned models of motion.
- Z continuously refines how the robot steers, accelerates, or repositions, rather than forcing a discrete on/off outcome.

- If sensor data shows a new obstacle mid-path, the system adapts the route proportionally—no abrupt stop unless absolutely required.

Output (Y)
- The evolving motor commands—velocity, joint angles, or rotation speeds.
- By preserving partial states, the robot can pivot from one trajectory to another with minimal energy loss, maintaining stability and safety.

Results and Benefits

Smoother Motion
Gradual course corrections replace harsh stops and starts, reducing mechanical wear and improving efficiency.

Adaptive Collision Avoidance
When partial obstacle data arrives, the system weighs it in real time and adjusts the path accordingly. The robot doesn't need to hit a hard threshold before reacting.

Fewer Configuration Changes
Conventional systems might cycle between multiple control modes (e.g., follow, avoid, wait). Binomial logic merges them into one fluid continuum, simplifying code and reducing latency.

Improved Scalability
As more sensors come online or tasks grow in complexity, the X–Z–Y approach naturally accommodates incremental data, rather than requiring an overhaul of discrete rule sets.

By moving beyond rigid binary triggers, binomial logic empowers robots to flow through their tasks. It delivers high reactivity, smooth path transitions, and robust performance in settings where pure on/off logic cannot keep pace with real-world nuances.

Financial Modelling

Overview

Financial markets are inherently dynamic and uncertain driven by shifting investor sentiment, global events, and complex economic indicators. Traditional computational models often rely on binary risk thresholds (e.g., "buy if above X," "sell if below Y"), forcing abrupt decisions that may miss subtle trends or accumulate false signals during volatile periods.

By applying Binomial logic to financial modelling, we replace these sharp buy/sell toggles with a flow-based approach. Here, the input (X) is market data (prices, volumes, economic indicators), the transformation (Z) is a dynamic matrix that continuously updates risk and sentiment factors, and the output (Y) is an evolving set of recommendations or positions rather than a simple on/off trade signal.

Implementation

Input (X)

- Live feeds of stock prices, technical indicators, real-time sentiment analysis (e.g., social media, news headlines), macroeconomic data.
- Instead of deciding "positive or negative" for each factor, X can hold partial influences (e.g., sentiment is 70% bullish, 30% uncertain).

Transformation (Z)

- A context-aware layer that integrates multiple signals (volatility measures, correlation among assets, global news "shock factors").
- Z adjusts in real time, shifting weight distributions. For instance, if global sentiment grows more cautious, Z incrementally reduces risky positions rather than waiting for a hard threshold.

Output (Y)

- Instead of a single buy/sell directive, Y is an adaptive strategy allocation adjustments, hedge ratios, partial scaling in or out of positions.
- When conditions remain uncertain, Y may hold a partial stance rather than all-in or all-out, protecting against large market swings.

Results and Benefits

Smoothed Decision Points

Rather than abrupt trades triggered by crossing a fixed line, the portfolio transitions more gracefully scaling exposure up or down in relation to subtle changes in indicators.

Lower Risk of False Alarms

In a purely binary model, one erroneous signal can trigger a major position change. Binomial logic weighs partial signals, lessening the chance of whipsaw trades on minor fluctuations.

Continuous Adaptation

As new data arrives (e.g., unexpected central bank decisions or sudden market sentiment shifts), the system adjusts instantly, without needing a formal re-parameterization of thresholds.

More Robust Portfolio Management

By holding partial stances, the system is inherently more diversified in its approach allocating resources in proportion to evolving confidence rather than making all-or-nothing calls.

Through Binomial logic, financial models move beyond the fragility of binary triggers, capturing the continuous nature of market behavior. This yields more adaptive, risk-aware strategies, reducing the probability of drastic missteps in turbulent market environments.

"Binomial logic doesn't force a verdict—it lets truth emerge like a seed learning how to grow."

Calculators and User Tools

Overview

Calculators and other user-facing computational tools typically rely on fixed arithmetic: the user enters a command, and the device follows a strict set of steps (addition, multiplication, etc.) in a sequential or "all-or-nothing" fashion. While this is fine for straightforward operations, it can limit flexibility—especially for more complex, multi-step problems or contexts where partial or dynamic inputs appear.

By embedding Binomial logic, calculators and user tools can transition from static, stepwise arithmetic to a flow-based system that reorders expressions intelligently, applies context-aware approximations, and refines results in real time. Here, X is the set of inputs or expressions entered by a user, Z is the adaptive layer that optimizes how calculations proceed, and Y is the final (but possibly continuously refined) result.

Implementation

Input (X)
- Could be a sequence of numbers, functions (log, sin, etc.), or even partial equations where some elements are not yet specified.
- In a typical binary setup, the calculator waits for the user to press "=", then yields a result. Binomial logic, however, can observe or interpret partial expressions before the "=" is pressed.

Transformation (Z)

- Reorders operations for efficiency (e.g., factoring out common denominators).
- Manages floating-point precision in real time, adjusting accuracy based on how many steps remain.
- Integrates user context (if the user is performing financial calculations, the tool might automatically handle currency rounding).
- Z does not simply run a single fixed formula; it learns from past inputs and user patterns, possibly presenting suggestions or clarifications mid-calculation.

Output (Y)

- The continuously updated result, which could refine itself if new data or new partial expressions are added by the user.
- Rather than a single freeze at "=," Y can highlight best approximations, dynamic re-checks, or warnings for potential rounding errors.

Results and Benefits

Optimized Computation

Especially for large or complex expressions, the system can reorder or group calculations to minimize the number of operations, saving time and potentially improving numerical stability.

Adaptive Precision

If the user only needs an approximate answer, binomial logic adjusts the accuracy early, preserving resources. If the user signals they need more exactness, it refines the result on the fly.

Context Awareness

A binomial-based calculator can detect patterns: if it sees frequent usage of certain financial formulas, it can pre-emptively format outputs or handle conversions automatically.

Enhanced User Experience

Partial or uncertain inputs (like placeholders or X variables) don't halt the system. The user can see real-time partial results, encouraging experimentation and incremental building of complex expressions.

Overall, Binomial logic elevates calculators and user tools from simple, discrete function executors to intelligent assistants that interpret context, reorder operations efficiently, and continuously adapt to user inputs providing a more fluid, interactive computational experience.

"Where Boolean declares, Binomial listens. Where Boolean breaks, Binomial bends."

Binomial Logic in Arduino

Overview

In conventional microcontroller systems, Boolean logic governs decision-making: 0 means false, 1 means true. While effective for digital switching, this rigid binary structure limits symbolic expression, context-awareness, and adaptive logic.

This Arduino-based experiment demonstrates how Binomial logic interpreting 0 as X and 1 as Y—can transform binary data from fixed states into relational symbols. By visualizing 8-bit representations of numbers using X and Y, the system showcases a symbolic, dynamic way to interpret logic at the hardware level.

Implementation

Input (X)
- Decimal numbers (0–9) were used as inputs.
- Each number was converted into an 8-bit binary representation.

Transformation (Z)
A simple substitution logic was used in the code:

#define X 0
#define Y 1
During output, every binary 0 was displayed as X, and every 1 as Y

The code used a displayXY() function to handle this transformation and print the result over the serial interface.

Output (Y)

The result was a stream of binomial values, such as:

Decimal: 5 | Binomial: XXXXXYXY

The output was symbolic, intuitive, and flexible—redefining binary states as fluid markers rather than fixed truths.

Code Snippet (Simplified)

```
#define X 0                          ⎫  DEFINE THE X AND
#define Y 1                          ⎬  Y VALUES
                                     ⎭

void displayXY(int value) {
    Serial.print("Decimal: ");
    Serial.print(value);
    Serial.print(" | Binomial: ");
    for (int i = 7; i >= 0; i--)
    {                                ⎫  PRINT THE
        int bitvalue = (value >> i) & 1;  ⎬  DECIMAL AND
        Serial.print(bitvalue == 0 ? 'X' : 'Y');  ⎭  BINOMIAL VALUE

    }
    Serial.println();
}
void setup() {                       ⎫  MCU SETUP
    Serial.begin(9600);              ⎬  FUNCTION
}                                    ⎭

void loop()
{
    for (int num = 0; num < 10; num++)  ⎫  ITERATE THROUGH
    {                                   ⎬  0-9 VALUE
    displayXY(num);                     ⎭
    delay(1000);
    }
}
```

110

Results and Benefits

Symbolic Representation
Binary values were expressed in a more human-readable, intuitive format—X and Y—encouraging symbolic reasoning.

Flexible Logic Encoding
By abstracting away from true/false logic, the system opened new possibilities for context-sensitive computation.

Hardware Simplicity
The experiment required only a basic Arduino and serial monitor, showing that binomial logic can be applied even in simple environments.

Foundations for Adaptive Processing
This approach could evolve toward more expressive, symbol-rich decision systems in IoT, AI, or edge computing applications.

Summary: Symbolic Thinking at the Hardware Level

This Arduino experiment redefined binary values by mapping 0 to X and 1 to Y, transforming fixed logic into symbolic flow. It offers a glimpse into how low-level systems can express Binomial logic opening doors to flexible encoding, intuitive interfaces, and the foundation of future adaptive computing models.

"Where Boolean logic draws a line, Binomial logic draws a connection."

Cognitive Numbers Theory – The Self-Cognitive "7"

Overview

Numbers typically appear as static symbols without agency. Cognitive Numbers Theory challenges that assumption by suggesting numbers can carry relational, interpretive meaning beyond their raw face value. In this scenario, "7" is treated as a "self-cognitive" entity—recognizing it exists in a numerical continuum and exploring how it relates to other numbers (like 6, 8, or 3.14...).

This is less about conventional math and more about how numbers gain context, identity, and adaptability in a binomial logic framework. While it may sound abstract or whimsical, it demonstrates how partial states and relational flows can apply even to seemingly rigid constructs like integers.

Input (X) – The Self-Cognitive "7"

- We imagine "7" not as a final value but as an ongoing question: "Who am I among other numbers?"
- This question arises from partial comparisons—7 is greater than 6 but less than 8, close to 7.0, distinct from 3.14 (π), etc.
- In standard Boolean logic, "7 = 7" is a tautology; there's no room for exploring how 7 might shift or be interpreted differently (e.g., in base 2, in a certain context, as 7.000).

Transformation (Z) – Cognitive/Context Layer
- In a binomial logic sense, Z stands for the interpretive matrix that weighs relational factors:
- Is "7" prime? (Yes, so it has unique significance among composite numbers.)
- Is "7" near a boundary condition? (7 is borderline for smaller subsets, e.g., a top 10 list?)
- Does "7" evoke cultural or psychological significance (lucky number in many traditions)?
- This transformation layer continuously updates how "7" is seen relative to other numeric contexts (in sets, ranges, expansions).

Output (Y) – Emergent Identity / Position
- As the system reevaluates data (additional comparisons, new frames of reference), "7" gains or refines its "identity."
- Instead of a static yes/no, the outcome might describe 7 as "the next integer after 6, prime, culturally significant, more stable than a fractional representation."
- If new contexts appear—like 7 on a temperature scale—Z might adapt the identity to "a mild warmth," or if 7 appears in a rating system (1 to 10), it's "above average."

Key Observations and Benefits

Partial State Preservation
- By letting "7" exist in flux, the system doesn't discard borderline comparisons. If we're unsure whether 7 is better classified with 6–9 or 3–7, we keep that possibility afloat until more data or context clarifies.

Context-Driven Meaning
- "7" in one domain (prime mathematics) has different resonance than in social contexts (a "lucky" or "favorite" number). The binomial logic approach to "unknowns" or partial states ensures

these interpretations can coexist, each transforming the identity of 7 differently.

Adaptive Logic
As new frames of reference or numeric sets are introduced, the transformation matrix Z evolves. So, if 7 is placed alongside irrational or complex numbers, the system updates how 7 is positioned—no abrupt toggles to "true/false," but a sliding interplay of relationships.

Bridging Subjective and Objective
Numerically, 7 is exact; cognitively, it can be considered special or typical depending on cultural or functional usage. Binomial logic merges these viewpoints—treating numeric absolutes and subjective meaning as part of a single continuum rather than a forced binary split.

Significance

This self-cognitive 7 illustration may seem playful, yet it highlights a deep principle: numbers aren't strictly lifeless or purely objective. They gain significance in how we interpret them—which set they belong to, what properties they share with neighbors, why they matter in a given context.

Under a Binomial logic lens:
- X is the numeric starting point (like "7"),
- Z is the evolving channel that weighs prime status, cultural beliefs, comparative sets, etc.,
- Y is the emergent role or identity that "7" claims at any point in time.

Where a traditional system might see "7 is 7, end of story," binomial logic and Cognitive Numbers Theory show fluid possibility: partial truths remain valid, continuous reinterpretation is allowed, and meaning emerges in real time. This approach can scale to more serious tasks like dynamic rating systems, algorithmic weighting, or personalized data interpretation blending arithmetic exactness with human-like relational context.

In Summary, the self-cognitive "7" case study demonstrates how Binomial logic can handle the interplay between abstract numeric identity and contextual interpretation—preserving partial states, bridging subjective and objective truths, and adapting continuously as new frames of reference enter the scene. It underscores that even something as seemingly cut-and-dry as a number can carry flexible meaning when examined through a relational, flow-based logic.

Internet of Things (IoT)

Overview

Traditional IoT systems rely heavily on discrete thresholds, such as "turn on the fan if the temperature exceeds 30°C" or "send an alert if motion is detected". While these binary (on/off) conditions work for simple automations, they often fail in dynamic environments. This rigidity can lead to overreactions, energy waste, or user frustration, as the system lacks the ability to interpret context and trends.

With Binomial Logic, IoT systems evolve into adaptive ecosystems. Inputs (X) from multiple sensors—temperature, motion, humidity, air quality—are no longer evaluated in isolation. Instead, a transformation layer (Z) dynamically maps interactions between inputs, considering contextual factors like time of day, occupancy patterns, and historical data. The system then produces outputs (Y) that reflect nuanced relationships, not just pre-set rules, leading to optimized comfort, energy efficiency, and responsiveness.

Implementation

Input (X)
Traditional IoT setups treat inputs independently, triggering actions when a specific value is reached. Binomial Logic interprets inputs relationally—for example, instead of simply detecting motion, it considers whether temperature is rising or whether the room was previously occupied.

Transformation (Z)

This layer processes data in real time to detect trends and interactions rather than individual triggers.

Example: If a room is gradually warming and occupied, Z may activate the fan at partial speed instead of abruptly turning on full cooling. If motion is detected in a cool room at night, Z may choose not to activate air conditioning but instead dim the lights for minimal disturbance.

Over time, Z can learn user habits and adjust responses accordingly.

Output (Y)

Instead of simple binary states, Y evolves dynamically based on X and Z.

Example: Adjusting fan speed proportionally, gradually dimming lights, or optimizing air filtration based on air quality trends.

Results and Benefits

Real-Time Adaptation

Devices respond not only to current sensor values but to patterns and trends, leading to more intelligent behavior.

Energy Efficiency

Avoids unnecessary activations—fans, AC units, and lights adjust only when there's a relational cause, reducing energy consumption.

Improved User Comfort

Systems anticipate user needs rather than reacting to rigid, pre-set triggers, creating a smoother and more intuitive experience.

Smarter Edge Processing

Reduces cloud dependency by enabling microcontrollers to make context-aware decisions locally using Binomial logic

Significance

Binomial logic transforms IoT from a collection of isolated sensors into a coherent network of responsive agents. Devices no longer flip between binary states but evolve their behavior through ongoing interaction. The result is a more intelligent, energy-conscious, and human-centric environment whether in smart homes, offices, or city infrastructures.

"Boolean splits the world into black and white. Binomial listens for the colors in between."

Appendix A

Custom Open License

Relational Binomial Computing System with Boolean Compatibility Version 1.0 – Released by Kannappan Chettiar

1. Grant of License

This license grants individuals, researchers, students, educators, and non-profit institutions the right to use, reproduce, and adapt the Relational Binomial Computing System with Boolean Compatibility ("the System") for non-commercial, educational, and research purposes.

2. Attribution

All use or adaptation of the System must include clear and visible attribution as follows:

"Based on the Relational Binomial Computing System developed by Kannappan Chettiar."

Attribution must appear in all publications, presentations, user interfaces, software documentation, and derivative works referencing or building upon the System.

3. Commercial Use

This license does not permit commercial use. For any for-profit application, sale, licensing, or integration of the System into commercial products or services, users must obtain prior written permission from the author and inventor. A separate commercial license agreement may apply.

4. No Claim of Ownership or Rebranding

Licensees may not claim ownership, inventorship, or exclusive rights over the System or its components.

Rebranding, renaming, or attempting to register the System or its foundational logic under alternative labels or trademarks is strictly prohibited.

5. Modification and Sharing

Users may adapt and share modified versions of the System for non-commercial use, provided that:

- Proper attribution is maintained (as outlined in Section 2)
- A clear notice of modification is included
- No endorsement by the original author is implied

6. No Warranty

The System is provided "as is", without warranty of any kind.
The author disclaims liability for any direct or indirect damages, errors, or consequences resulting from its use or misuse.

7. License Updates

This license may be revised in the future to enhance clarity or respond to evolving use. Updated versions will be made available through official channels.

8. Contact for Commercial Licensing or Partnerships

To request commercial use, collaboration, or integration:
✉ kc@switchingbattery.com
🌐 www.kannappanchettiar.com.

Stay Connected & Explore More

Thank you for taking the time to read this book. If you found the ideas here thought-provoking or want to dive deeper into Binomial Computing, I'd love to connect.

I actively share updates, projects, and insights across different platforms. Whether you're interested in collaborating, discussing the concepts in this book, or just following my work, feel free to reach out:

GitHub – Explore related projects, code, and contributions:
https://github.com/KannappanChettiar

Website – Learn more about my work, research, and latest updates:
www.kannappanchettiar.com | www.masterkannappan.com

LinkedIn – Connect with me professionally and join the conversation:
https://www.linkedin.com/in/kannappanchettiar/

About the Author

Kannappan Chettiar is a Quantum Flow Strategist who simplifies complexity by aligning technology with the natural intelligence of flow. He is the creator of XY Binomial Logic, Cognitive Numbers Theory, Node Fusion Technology and Switching Battery—new frameworks that redefine computation, AI, and energy through relational thinking.

As the Founder of the Switching Battery, powered by Node Fusion Technology, he has translated quantum theory into practical breakthroughs in renewable energy—designing systems that adapt, balance, and optimize in real time flow.

With double master's degrees in law from University of California, Berkeley and National University of Singapore, and degrees in finance and education, Kannappan bridges disciplines to challenge the limits of artificially imposed intelligence and advocates for a return to intuitive, nature-based decisioning process based on Quantum Flow Intelligence.

This book reflects his mission: to move beyond rigid logic into a world where systems flow, intelligence evolves, and technology becomes truly alive.

"Boolean logic chooses sides.
Binomial logic finds balance."

.